Here's what ac
Blessed", now a movi
Leif Gregersen's writi

"Every once in a blessing while, a voice comes out of nowhere that astonishes you with its vulnerability and courage. Leif Gregersen is this voice for me. I pray "Through The Withering Storm" finds its way to those grappling with mental illness so they can see that they are not alone and that there is support out there, and I pray that this book finds its way into the homes of those families who are trying to find insight into what is happening to someone they love who is battling a mental illness. This book is one I will return to time and time again for humility and empathy. Thank you, Leif, for your courage, and for sharing your story.

-Richard Van Camp, former Writer-In-Residence for the University of Alberta

Purchase "Through The Withering Storm" and "Green Mountain Road" online and read free stories from the author as well as following his blog at www.valhallabooks.com

Hope you enjoy the parts of this you haven't read yet. I am very proud that you have been so supportive of my writing.

Leif Gregersen
11 July 2013

Table of Contents:

Chapter One

The two brothers sat transfixed by the warm glow of the campfire. Despite it being daytime, the fire was warmth. The fire was a place to cook their food and the fire was also a symbol of unity between the two. The older brother, Steve, had taught the younger, Colin, many of the ways of the wilderness – the same wilderness that he so cherished growing up in the mountains of the interior of British Columbia. There was a cool late winter breeze flowing through the treetops above them that gave them a sense that the world was far away and mostly unimportant, compared to the bonds of love and family right in the here and now. The two, though born nine years apart, shared a bond that seemed neither time or distance could ever break. They could talk about anything that was on the young 10-year-old Colin's mind. The 19-year-old Steve never tired of bringing his younger brother out like this, even on this special day when Steve's girlfriend was with them. The elder of the two Hansen brothers would never imagine leaving his brother behind. Little Colin was his inspiration to walk the path of honesty and clean living. And Steve knew that he was the hero, the inspiration in young Colin's life to do everything from outwit his bullies to being as smart and mature as he was despite his limited years.

"Colin, do you think you can make yourself scarce when Lisa gets back? Just for a little while. You can go down to the waterfront and look for rocks and stuff, can't you? Just don't go on the ice, though. It's already pretty thin."

"Sure, Stevie. You're going to get all kissie-faced again with her, aren't you?" Colin asked, as he made a face like he had just sucked a lemon.

"It's a little more than that, little man, but I'm hopeful. Here, check this out." Steve held out a small jewelry box with a ring in it for Colin to see.

"Wowwww!" Colin said, clearly impressed. "Are you going to give that to Lisa? Grandma used to have one of those. What is it?"

"Actually, it's Grandma's. I asked Mom for it and now I'm going to propose to Lisa with it." Steve replied.

"Propose? What does that mean?"

"Colin, my boy, do you know how you become an uncle?"

"I'm not really sure. Are you an uncle when you get to be drinking buddies with someone's dad?" Colin asked, with a bit of confusion on his face.

"No, you get to be an uncle when your brother or sister has a baby." Steve's words left Colin a bit stunned.

"Wow, are you going to have a baby? I thought only girls could do that." Colin said innocently.

"I'll tell you a bit more when we get home, okay? For now, Lisa and I just need some time alone for a little while. Hey, here she comes now. Just let us have a few minutes. Then you can come back, okay?"

"Sure, Stevie. I'll do it." Colin replied. He would do anything for his older brother, even walk around confused until the kid in school who giggles a lot and kind of smells fills him in.

"What are you guys talking about?" asked the beautiful young Lisa who looked at the two faces grinning at her as she returned from a visit to the bushes. "Are you two up to something again?"

"Maybe." Young Colin said.

"Alright, geniuses. Spill it. What's up?" Lisa demanded.

"Ah, Colin and I were just having a very serious discussion. You see, I seem to think that Batman has more money than Uncle Scrooge and Colin disagrees."

"Oh, I see. The age-old debate. What makes me think you're full of it? What's really up?"

"Well, for starters, our little Colin here is going to have a problem unless he excuses himself." Steve said as he shooed Colin away from himself.

"Okay, okay. I got to go. I'll be back in a little while." Colin declared. As he turned to go, Lisa smiled her bright, warm smile at Stevie and leaned down to give him a passionate kiss.

"Now that he's gone, we can get down to business." Stevie said.

"Business? I thought we agreed we were going to get down to that kind of business less until we had our own place?" Lisa replied.

"Hey, Colin!" Stevie shouted as he remembered. "Stay off that ice and keep in sight!" Then he said quietly to Lisa, "Well, let's just say we have things to discuss." As he said that, Lisa seemed to lose a bit of her happy demeanor and her faced looked somber.

As for Colin, he left the warmth and comfort of the fire and walked down to the lakefront in the late winter/early spring sun. Despite that it was an awful feeling being left out of something, Colin enjoyed having a little time off to his own. All his young life he loved to explore, to embrace the beauty of the lake and the mountains and everything that surrounded him in this nearly untouched area as only a child could. Colin and Steve and their parents lived in what he believed, despite his young years, to be the most beautiful place on the planet. It was a small community known as Walker Lake nestled in what everyone called the BC interior and, even at this time of year, the evergreen trees were proud and beautiful and the snow on the mountain peaks made for awe-inspiring scenery. Colin could sit for hours just staring and never get bored of any of it.

Back at the campfire, Colin's brother was trying to find the best way to ease into the question he was about to ask his girlfriend Lisa.

"Lisa, I brought you here to ask you something…to tell you something…ummm, I don't really know how to approach this. We've been seeing each other for a couple of really good years and…"

"Stevie, don't keep me in suspense!" Lisa answered, sounding a bit worried.

"I think I know a secret that you don't know I know." He looked into Lisa's eyes and saw more worry and fear than he was comfortable with. It hurt him deep down that she was even thinking that what he was about to say was bad news. She couldn't hold his gaze and looked down, covered her face with her hand and sobbed. "Hey-hey! What's this all about? Why are you sad?" Steve asked with compassion, feeling sympathy at her reaction.

"It's about the baby isn't it? I knew I shouldn't have told Smitty. I feel so bad. I was really careful. I'll do what you want. I made an appointment. I'm going to fly out and get the abortion next week." she said, sheepishly.

"Abortion!" Steve exclaimed. "Are you nuts? Why would you want an abortion?"

"You don't want an abortion?" Lisa said, sounding surprised.

"Of course not! I want to be a father. I want to marry you! I love you, Lisa. I've always wanted to have a child, maybe a few children. I'll work hard, I'll treat you right. I'm not some loser who gets what he wants and moves on. This is me. I love you. I want to be with you forever!"

"Here!" Steve thrust out the jewelry box without much ceremony and opened it for her. When she saw the ring, her mouth gaped open wide and she flung her arms around him. Many times in their relationship, Lisa had felt she had made some grave mistakes that would end things but, time and again, Steve would prove to her that he was a kind and caring person and that she deserved to be treated right. Maybe it was immaturity, but Lisa wanted so bad to please him. She saw him as not only a strong and handsome partner but also such a good person. In all she had seen of him the past two years, she was ready to accept even a lifetime commitment without much prompting even though there were a few nagging doubts. After all, doesn't everyone have some trepidation about taking such a big step?

"Stevie, are you nuts? The rest of our lives is a very long time. So much could happen. I could change-you could change." Lisa was trying to stop the tears that were flowing down her face. Steve had a hard time telling if they were tears of joy or tears of desperation.

"Lisa, listen to me. We can do this any way you want. We can have a long engagement. We can try living together for a while. This ring, even though it means something as a family heirloom, just means that I love you enough to stick around and I'll go through anything with you. And the baby that's on the way, I want to love it, to raise it, to take care of you and him or her – forever "

"Steve, it's just that we're so young. I just finished high school a year ago. I don't know what I want to do with my life. This isn't the first time I've been pregnant. I…"

"Lisa, listen to me." Stevie said, stopping her by grasping her shoulders as though he was going to shake some sense into her. "I know about the past, I want to prove to you that I can make up for it. Not all guys are bad. You hooked up with a few bad apples and had your problems. I love you, Lisa! I love you when I see you help with Colin. I love when we talk for hours on the phone. And for whatever reason, I love you even more that there is a baby-our baby-growing in you. To me, it's like our love created a whole new human being that's going to depend on us totally and love us unconditionally. We've all been through tough times, but we can get through if we're together. Without you in my life, there would be really no point in going on. I need you Lisa.

Now, here," he said, taking out the ring again, "Lisa, will you marry me and share your life with me?"

"The rest of my life? What about college? What about a place to live and a place to raise our baby? What happens when a year or two goes along and you decide you want something else? Have you thought of all that?"

"Maybe not all of it but a lot of it. For starters, I'm not going to college. I want to stay here in Walker Lake where I can be home with you every night and our baby. Smitty and I are going to start a business and we're ready to put in the hard work we need to make it grow. As for a place to live, I know we can stay with my family for a while and I've got a job at the sawmill so I can put money away for us to get an apartment soon enough. And our families will help. Do you understand that you've been all I wanted since the ninth grade? I thought it was just a crush at first but it worked out into so much more. There hasn't been a day since then that I haven't thought about you, about how you care about every one of God's creatures from goldfish to humans. I love the way you can smile and make anything bad I could think about float away. And, then, I finally get you and there is now this beautiful new creation that I love already growing inside you. Can't you understand it can be everything we talked about-dreamed about?"

"I just need some time, Stevie. I need to think. I need to talk to my parents. I need to sort this out in my head."

"And I wouldn't want you to make this decision without them. I'll wait as long as it takes. My love for you won't go away and I have a pretty good feeling your love for me won't either."

With that, they moved closer together and kissed with the intense passion of youth. He knew it was a bit naughty but Steve took his hand and put it around her back and up and under her jacket, under her shirt. He searched her back for the scar he knew would be there. She had the scar since she was young, a burn scar from a camping trip. There was something so attractive to Steve about it, something flawed yet beautiful. For whatever reason, it was his favorite part of her.

"Are you fondling my scar again, Stevie?" Lisa asked coyly.

"No way," Steve replied, "I'm innocent. I was just trying to get your bra off."

"Well, at least you're being honest." She smiled, looking into his eyes. "I guess we're pretty much past the point of getting the milk for free." Lisa said, unzipping her jacket, revealing under a thin t-shirt a slim and healthy figure that could drive any man wild. Steve didn't want to mention that her body was another thing on the list that he loved about her but not just because she was so shapely, but because, since they had first officially been a couple, she had kept herself only for him. She reached back, pushing out her chest, and undid her bra strap. Stevie started to feel the energy of desire run through him and went to assist her in undressing. Normally, she felt self-conscious about such a thing but she knew her body was an object of great desire for Steve and just about any healthy grown male. Now that she had someone to completely give herself to, it only made sense to cap off this moment with a bit of real passion. Then, the yell came.

"Stevie!" Colin's voice came loudly and with a bit of an echo. "This ice isn't thin at all!"

"Shit!" Stevie spat as he snapped out of the passionate moment they were in. "Colin's out on the lake. That damn ice is going to break! Sorry, Lisa. I better go get him."

"It's okay", Lisa said. "I wouldn't have you do anything else. But we're not bringing him on our honeymoon!"

"Well, then, who are we gonna get to chop wood for us?" Steve said as he smiled and quickly looked all around himself for something. His eyes settled on a long and strong looking dry stick that was on the ground. He grabbed it, ran off down to the lake's edge. It was difficult for Lisa to get her head around what was now happening but deep down inside she had faith in Stevie. He always seemed to know what to do, what would save the day. She felt such a feeling of love and pride that this was her man, this was the guy who would provide for her and protect her for the rest of her life. In a couple of minutes after she had composed herself, Lisa followed him down to the lakefront. Colin was about 40 feet onto the ice.

"Colin!!" Steve snapped. "Get the hell back here but carefully. That ice is way too thin! A notice was in the paper, some of it won't hold ten pounds! Get down on your belly nice and easy and crawl back!"

"Okay Stevie, I'm coming!" Colin leaned down and, for just a moment, rested all of his weight on one leg. Steve heard a sharp crack from the ice and followed by a sudden 'sploosh.' The ice had broken beneath Colin and he was in the freezing water.

"Colin!!!" Steve screamed. He could have been a thousand miles away. Colin was under the water and couldn't hear him. Steve kept his head and got down on all fours, carrying the stick he had found. A few seconds later, Colin, a good swimmer for his age, popped back above the surface of the hole he had fallen into. The best swimmer in the world though would know they had to get him out of that cold water or he would freeze to death in mere minutes.

"Stevie! Help!" Colin screamed, flailing for dear life.

"Hold on, Colin, hold on! Try not to freak out!" Steve replied in a clear, loud voice. "Keep dog paddling. I'll get to you."

"It's cold, Stevie! Hurry!" Stevie knew he didn't have much time but soon he was closing in to where Colin was. When he got in close enough, he extended the stick so Colin could grab it, and, once he did, pulled for all he was worth.

"Hold tight, Colin. Don't let go!" Steve yelled as his poor frozen little ice-pop brother slid upwards and out of the hole in the ice. "Now, hold onto that stick so I can pull you in. The ice around that hole is still pretty..." Crack. The ice under Stevie collapsed, who was much heavier than the 10-year-old Colin. Lisa screamed but Steve adeptly swam up to the surface. When he got there, he dog-paddled and cracked the ice with his hands off towards the shore, until he got to a point where he could ease himself up on more solid ice. He soon got back on dry land and coached his freezing little brother in. As soon as everyone was safe, despite his own approaching hypothermia, he grabbed Colin, hugged him and carried him, rubbing his exposed parts, loosening his wet clothes to be taken off when they got to the fire. Lisa raced ahead of them. She was confused and almost in a state of panic, not knowing what to do until Stevie sent her to stoke up their fire and get blankets from the car.

Over the next couple of hours, the two warmed themselves up, tried to dry their clothing, feasted on hot dogs, and laughed about the whole incident as most do. None of them were indestructible – their demise could come from anywhere, at any time, whether they be brave, vigilant, loved or hated.

As they walked back to their vehicle, Colin ran on ahead and Lisa whispered into Steve's ear, "That was the bravest, most awesome thing I've ever seen. Give me that ring now. I would be stupid not to marry a man like you." Steve smiled and reached into his pocket but there was no ring. For a moment his heart stopped and then he realized it was in the waterproof coat he put around Colin. As they warmed up the truck, Steve said very little and put the ring on Lisa's finger, looked into her loving, glowing eyes and gave her a simple kiss on the lips. That was all that was needed.

Chapter Two

Colin, Steve and Lisa drove back to the trailer the two boys shared with their parents up Green Mountain Road and tried not to worry about what their parents might say if they found out about the whole ice thing. When they got in the door, the two boys left Lisa to chat with their parents while they changed their still damp clothing. When they returned, their mother looked at them suspiciously and said "Stevie, I think you have something you want to tell me."

Crap, Steve thought to himself. What had given it away? Then he remembered that Lisa was wearing the ring he had given her. Before he could say much, his mom got up and hugged the stuffing out of him, saying: "I wish your grandmother was here to see this." Steve's mom tried to hide the tears welling up in her eyes, glancing back at her husband who remained silent. She stepped back and looked into her son's eyes and said, "Are you sure you understand exactly what you're getting yourself into, son?"

"I have never been..."
"We..." Lisa said.

"We...have never been more sure of anything, Mom." Steve said, gathering up his courage to make the sentence he had just spoken sound as bold as possible. The statement was followed by a few more seconds of awkward silence.

"Mom...Dad...I have something else to tell you. Lisa and I...well, Lisa...umm...Let's just say you two better get used to the idea of being grandparents pretty quick."

There were a few more awkward moments of silence as that news sunk in.

"Stevie, is that why you and Lisa want to get married? I hope you understand that there is a lot more to a lifetime commitment than having a baby." His mom had a worried look on her face.

"No, Mom, that's not why. Lisa and I have felt this way about each other for a long time, maybe since we first laid eyes on each other back in grade nine."

After a few moments, Steve realized that his dad wasn't showing any sign of reaction. It was an uncomfortable silence that triggered a fear of being berated or even beaten, as the boy's father had been known to do at times. Uneasy and unsure, Steve held his breath. Finally, his dad spoke. "Are you sure you two are ready for this? Do you even have a clue of what you're getting into?" At these words, Steve's stomach churned.

"Ready or not it's going to happen." Steve replied, smiling.

"What about money? You're not even working right now. And what about college?"

"I'm not sure about college right now and I'm going to work at the mill just like you do. I talked to the foreman already and he said I can start any time." Steve stood more confidently now, having armed himself with a partial plan for responding to his father in this type of situation.

"I have some things figured out. Smitty and I are going to start an adventure tour company. Bungee jumping, hunting and fishing tours. We're going to advertise on the Internet, take people out and show them God's Country, the way you showed us and the way I'm showing Colin, plus what we learned over the years. We can't miss. The economy is great and we've done some research. A lot of big city Americans come up here, just dying for a chance to hunt or fish in a place that hasn't been completely depleted. A lot of them pass Walker Lake right by, not knowing what they're missing. If we could just pull in three, four tourists a week, we'll be rolling in cash," Steve said with a glimmer of hope in his voice that this wasn't just another idea his dad was going to shoot down and laugh at.

"Stevie, let's let your mother and Lisa chat right now and take a little walk." As they got out in the yard, the senior Hansen let out what seemed to have been boiling inside him since the topic had been brought up. "Yes, you can miss, Stevie," his Dad said, stressing the more childish version of his name. "And you can jeopardize all the money you've saved, not to mention the well-being of your wife and child."

"Don't worry, Dad! I've thought it all through. We talked it over with Smitty's dad and he's an accountant. Remember? He likes the idea, He says it's sound, and says he'll back us up, possibly even help us get a grant – not a loan, a grant, meaning we won't have to pay it back. We'll work full-time with you in the sawmill until our company gets busy enough to go full-time."

His father considered Steve's words. He sighed.

"Well, I suppose you've made your bed and you can lie in it. I won't even get into how you're making a big mistake. If you want to have a baby, why not put this child up for adoption and then establish yourself so you're really ready to have a family and a marriage?"

"Dad, you don't understand!" Steve said, beginning to raise his voice and feel the frustration and embarrassment he seemed to always have with his father. "This is my life now, I'm ready for this. Lisa and I love each other. We're not going to jump into marriage but we definitely aren't going to abort or give up our baby."

"Well, Stevie, what do you think might have happened to you and Colin and your mother here if I had chased some unproven plan? It's a good plan, I'll give you that. Hell, you can do whatever you want. I'll even help you as I can. You have to realize though you're running a good chance of ending up working in a sawmill with two missing fingers and a crappy old pickup for the rest of your life. Or, working as a truck driver, never seeing your family ten months out of the year, if you don't go to college and get some marketable skills. Right now, all seems like roses and honey but life can kick your ass if you let it."

Steve wanted to storm out, to hide from all the advice his dad had ever given him but the old guy looked sincere, even a little sad and concerned. It did make sense but there was no way he was ready to give up on marriage and family and the loving arms of this beautiful young woman he had chosen. Part of him said he would never get another chance at college and the rest of him was on fire with love that filled his whole being and passion that cemented in his love for Lisa. All he could say was, "I'll think about what you've said." It was a way to pacify his father. Steve excused himself and went in to get Lisa so he could take her home.

On the way, he asked her if she would mind taking off her ring when she got there. They both agreed that it would be best if he came back tomorrow and they could tell her parents about everything then.

As they were about to part, the young couple and their child-to-be held each other just as close as they could, except Lisa had a hard time resisting temptation and put her hand on her lover's right inner thigh and slid her hand up until she made contact with Steve's pleasure zone. Knowing it would be hard to have real privacy anywhere but here, Steve pulled the truck over and touched Lisa's chin as she massaged his hardening sex organ. She stopped as he whispered the word, 'wait' to her and he turned her head up so he could look in her eyes.

"You're the most beautiful thing I've ever known and I'll love you no matter what until the day I die. I love having sex with you but you don't need to. I've been thinking a lot about what my dad said. It makes some sense but I promise you I'll be there for you no matter what."

With those words, Lisa turned her head down as though she were ashamed and began to sob.

"Lisa, what is wrong? Everything is so right for us. We're going to have a good life together."

"I just can't...I can't..." She had a hard time forming the words she wanted to tell him.

"Tell me. What could be wrong?"

"I love you, Stevie. I love you so much. When I see you being a sort of surrogate father to Colin and when you say these kind things to me, it makes me love you even more. I know that you are a good, decent person. But it just seems in my life that if anything good happens, it backfires on me. Nothing stays this good forever. You say you love me but you don't know about my past. I used to have this boyfriend and he was a bad man but I loved it. I didn't love him but I loved being a rebel, until he started to think I was cheating on him and he started to beat me so I broke up with him and he stalked me. I was so scared, I didn't think I would make it. I don't think I deserve all this. You, your family, your big plans and friends that would do anything for you."

"Sweetheart, I said I loved you and I meant it. I love you no matter what, no matter when, no matter who. If one day we have to leave this town, things will work themselves out. Now, look at me." He took her head in his hands and brought her gaze up to his. The glow of love and sensuality was so strong when he looked at her, he couldn't imagine for a second she didn't feel the same thing. After a few moments of looking into Lisa's eyes, he moved in for a deep, longing kiss and he felt his excitement grow as she responded to his probing tongue. They let passion take over. There was no world outside, just perfect mutual pleasure in each other as their two young fit bodies united.

Fortunately, the truck was wide enough for the two of them to lay down on top of each other. Steve had pulled off his shirt and then his pants as Lisa undressed. Their passion was clumsy but unforgettable because they had finally gotten to the point where they could both love and express love without fear. He could tell that something was growing inside of her – her flat stomach was just beginning to have a bit of roundness and that excited him all the more. No action, no pleasure, no drug, no drink could have brought him more pure ecstasy than that moment when two were complete for just a moment. When Stevie finally finished, he didn't want to leave the intimacy of being inside her and they lay together joined for the next few minutes until they finally pulled apart and reluctantly got back into their clothes.

"Stevie..." Lisa asked softly.
"Yes, lover..." he replied.
"Do you believe in God?"
"Of course I do. Since I was little."
"I heard once that, all our lives, we are like Adam and Eve until we find our perfect mate, perfect lover, perfect love all in one and, in that union, life for those two are made perfect. You made the earth move for me, you know."

"It was awesome for me, too. In not too long, we'll be able to say goodnight and not have to go home afterwards. To me, that's heaven." Lisa embraced him closely and despite that they had no more lovemaking strength, the two connected in a way better than in a sexual way and they stared out the window of the truck at the stars and the moon-lit mountains. They talked for a long time about who their baby would be more like and the things they wanted to do with him or her when the child was born. An hour, maybe two went by as they held each other and talked and, when Steve dropped her off, Lisa walked into her parent's home feeling like she was on a cloud. As Steve drove home, he too felt like he wanted to shout out to the world that he had a girl that loved him and a girl that he loved. It made him a little reckless and he drove a little faster than he should have but, in a way, that was celebrating for him. That was how he let the world know that he felt on top of it.

When Lisa got in the door, her parents were up and waiting for her. Her Mother was a caring woman but often silent around Lisa's father. They could tell she was happy, deeply happy. They hadn't seen her like this for a long time.

"Lisa honey," her mother queried. "What's got into your head coming home at this hour?"

"Mom, Dad..." she felt almost like she was about to tell them she had won the lottery. "Steve and I are going to have a baby." With that her Dad walked over and said nothing, making Lisa feel almost like she was going to get hit, and her Mother sat in her chair as tears ran down her face. Her Dad came up and hugged her which threw her off guard at first, but then she told herself she had done nothing wrong. Lisa and her parents stayed up late that night, talking and laughing, planning and in a glow of happiness.

Within the next few days, Lisa was pretty much living at the Hansen household full-time. At first, Steve's dad didn't agree. But, in the end, he realized that if he lectured further and forbade this and forbade that it would just turn his son away and maybe even his own wife that seemed to be caring more about her new daughter than her old husband. Frank Hansen just wished there was some way he could show his eldest boy what he was getting into. He thought back to the days before he had met Steve's mother and how the world had beaten him down. He had met a young woman at that early time in his life and was devastated when she turned down his marriage proposal for no apparent reason, then went on to marry some rich person she barely knew. Life can be a cold, hard place, he thought, but he couldn't bring himself to pop Steve's balloon of happiness.

Over the next few weeks, Steve, Lisa and his parents were kept busy, making trips to the library, looking at plans and different permits they would need for the various structures, canoe racks and other items that were necessary for their business. They also had to price out tools and find time in between to work with Smitty and his accountant father on a business plan. Smitty and Steve also set themselves up to work at the sawmill where Steve's dad was employed at and began working eight hours a day, feeding seemingly endless amounts of wood into saws that were less than forgiving. The harsh reality of working in a sawmill is that people lose fingers, arms, even their lives but having a steady pay cheque going into the Hansen household was sorely needed, especially with a baby on the way.

All of them were careful to get enough sleep at night so they could carry on their jobs safely. Lisa helped a lot by teaching Steve some of the yoga moves she had learned to prepare him for his difficult days. Then, when he came home, she would give him a massage and put him into a hot bath and wash his clothes. These were just simple things but done with a kindness that made Steve feel deep down inside that, when he and Lisa were joined forever in marriage, they would make a great team.

Lisa was seen as a welcome addition to the family from Steve's parents because she often helped her potential mother-in-law with cooking, cleaning and other chores in between reading up on pregnancy and child development books. Little did they know that Lisa had made top marks in school for her sauces and gravies and desserts. She made a lot of these for the family and most of it was incredible. Steve, ever the ambitious entrepreneur, decided that part of his tours would be a meal cooked by his beautiful and talented fiancée.

Despite all the work they had to do, on the weekends they kept activities down to just what the whole family could do together. In the evenings, everyone was usually buried in a book with the exception of Colin who was working his way through a stack of comics. Steve's father's negative attitude and grumpiness still reared its head from time to time, but even he had to admit that things seemed to be looking up for all of them.

All the ambition and activity around him made Frank rethink a goal he had for a long time. The Hansen property was almost 13 acres and, for quite some time, he had been turning around an idea of building a house near the back of the lot that would suit his family better and add value to his property while giving himself something to do that he enjoyed. He had gotten as far as clearing an area for the house and he had friends that helped him get the plot ready for utilities, but he figured that Steve could now lend a hand and would benefit from more room to himself. He started to get serious about the work.

While Steve had his catalogs of adventure equipment and small business books ranging from accounting to advertising to general success and motivation books and CDs, Frank could spend hours absorbed in handyman and woodworking books. His goal was to produce a house that was warmer, more efficient and more comfortable than any he had seen. So many times, as a younger man, he had been on construction crews and built houses that sold for more than twice what a regular place would, not just for location, but for sheer luxury, and he always personally resented that he had built so many and worked with millions of board feet of lumber but, he himself, lived in a cheaply constructed trailer.

While Steve's best friend, Smitty, tried to get a head start on the English courses he would be taking in university, Lisa and Steve's mom would knit, sew and read books about pregnancy, child rearing and whatever else they could find in town. With the rapidly approaching end of nine months of pregnancy, Steve's mom was happier than she had been in years, believing that now she had a chance to do right what she didn't know enough of to have done with her own boys or, at the least, try to keep Lisa from making the mistakes she did with Steve and Colin. Steve's Mom was like Lisa in that way. She blamed herself for problems her children had while her husband Frank was far from being perfect himself. Perhaps, the two were attracted to each other as more than just daughter-in-law to mother-in-law because of the way that characteristic worked out. She was glad to see Steve not be like that. As for her opinion of Lisa, she often thought a lot of young women could be apprehensive to take such instructions as she was giving her, from a mother-in-law, but Lisa proved herself to be a gracious and appreciative student.

Some of the things she was told, of course, were old wives tales and superstitions, but even these had their place. As in the homes of many Danish families, the kitchen in their trailer had a 'witch' doll on a little broom hanging from the ceiling that was supposed to help cakes from falling or worse. Then, there was the Danish way of eating nearly every kind of cheese and small seafood from smoked oysters to Plaice on an open-faced rye bread sandwich. There were many traditions but a lot of them were now saved for Christmas which was possibly going to be right around the time of Lisa's due date. Steve often spoke of the present his fiancée was going to give him and how it would be better than anything he could ever ask for.

Lisa drank in all the odd little Danish traditions, believing that, without these little fun things, people would lose their sense of identity and kids would lose their feeling that the world was the fascinating and magical place that it should be to them. Even though he was getting a bit old for a lot of it, it was still a joy for all the Hansens to tell Colin stories and make the last years before his teens as magical as possible.

Smitty couldn't let his dad or himself down with regards to post-secondary education, which wasn't all bad. They had anticipated the winter months to be slower in the Rocky Mountain paradise they all called home, so they decided Smitty could just work four months in the summer with the regular tours helping Steve and, then, he could leave the community for school during the other eight. Smitty didn't really need to work in the sawmill with Steve. He had bonds and savings accounts given to him from his parents, totaling much more than he could earn, but he did, partly because he wanted to show Steve he was willing to work towards something, and partly because he hated the idea of being a privileged rich kid who would one day know a lot about books and the profession he chose but nothing about how to really get down and work on something practical, like adding his own personal touches to his home or to be able to camp and hunt and fish.

One day, while they were working on the new house, Smitty brought forth the idea that in slow times, if it were built large enough, they could turn the house into a Bed and Breakfast, bringing in income and, if it were run right, bringing in customers who wanted to see the Rockies and could be sold on ice fishing tours or cross-country skiing trips as well. He spoke to his father about it and he told Frank he could get him a partial grant for the cost of the project and that was the first time in awhile the boys had seen him truly happy.

As the weeks passed, the ice on the rivers and lakes receded and the mountain streams began to flow with fresh clean water from the melting ice and snow in higher elevations. In some ways, the mountains were still a treacherous place with their cold winds and cliffs and rock faces, but they became more and more of a thing of beauty as the spring flowers bloomed and the deep, rich green of the foliage began to fill in spaces between the pines. There was so much color and life: from the multitude of birds to the marmots and mountain squirrels and even the odd bear, more afraid of settlements than outsiders realized but still forced out of their hibernation cycle to return to the world outside their den and gather food and raise their cubs.

Often, a moose or mountain goat could be seen from the road and, sadly, now and then someone would hit them with their vehicle and be lucky if they survived to tell the tale.

It was times like these when you could walk past bushes full of flowers with their scent sweeter than the finest perfume and see all the crystal clear streams cut through the melting snow and ice that they all loved to embrace the most. The family would take time out of their day and, in a group, walk through the pines to witness the greatness of the mountains and the power of nature. It was such a perfect opportunity for all of them to get together as a real family and share whatever was on their hearts with each other, even getting some essential exercise.

Inside the Hansen trailer, life anew was coming forth much as the Rocky Mountain region of British Columbia, Canada, renewed itself again as it had done for more years than any scientist or preacher could honestly say for sure. Lisa's baby bump was growing more visible as the days became longer and warmer.

Even young Colin seemed to mature beyond his few years as he took on such tasks as carrying tools and nails and wood for his father's projects in the yard. He was starting to understand what it was to be an uncle and he liked the idea of setting an example for someone younger. He even looked forward to the concept of not being 'the baby' anymore.

One day, Steve's mom woke up with a headache that was a good deal worse than normal. Colin was at school and the other Hansens were working. It was a fair walk to town but a nice and sunny day to do it in. Without thinking much of it, Colin's mother sent Lisa down Green Mountain Road to get some acetaminophen with codeine, the only stuff that helped when she had these headaches, and this was definitely a bad one. She thought nothing of it until hours passed and Lisa hadn't phoned or returned. For a while, Ruth made excuses to herself that she hadn't explained to Lisa how important it was to get the pills soon or that maybe she stopped for coffee. Then, when more time passed, the possibility that she went to the sawmill to see Stevie and catch a ride came up but when the men returned, there was no Lisa. Soon, panic and paranoia began to set in, ever so slightly at first, but it grew worse as the hours and minutes rolled by and phone calls didn't give them any answers. Finally, they decided that they all had best get looking for her. Nothing could have prepared them for what they were soon to discover.

Chapter Three

Each member of the Hansen family foresaw their own private nightmare of what had happened to Lisa. She was never late like this and, in her condition, there was twice the reason to be concerned. The first thing the two elder Hansen males did was to drive down Green Mountain Road slowly and carefully, looking for any sign that might indicate what was going on, and also looking for the sight they didn't want to see – Lisa incapacitated and beyond help. They didn't have a cell phone so there was no way to communicate with police or Smitty or anyone else who could help with the search, so they left Ruth back at the trailer to keep phoning around to anyone who may have seen Lisa and to stay near the phone in case something did come up. When their truck lumbered into Walker Lake proper, Frank volunteered to go on foot while Colin and Steve went to get Smitty and any others who might be able to help.

Frank set out to cover as much territory as he could. Up and down the main streets of the small but spread-out town with its erratic streets and deeply sloping hills and valleys he walked, letting all the worst scenarios play out in his mind. He could only imagine what was playing out in Steve's mind. As he searched, Frank thought about how he had really started to like the idea of having a baby grandchild in the house. It made him think back to what it was like when Steve and Colin were little: the feeling of completeness and pride, and the incredible capacity of children to love unconditionally. The eldest Hansen hadn't felt comfortable around children except his own. He had also been starting to feel some pride in the fact that his son really was working hard and dedicating himself to his family and his family-to-be.

It was Frank who found Lisa around an hour later, curled up on the sidewalk and holding her chest and coughing. It looked as though she had tried to walk but couldn't, as there was a trail of blood ten feet long leading up to her curled up form. It was an extremely disturbing sight to come across, the happy and giving young woman who was soon to be a very welcome new member of his family, crying and bruised, curled up on the ground. Frank felt badly for her but felt worse for what it would do to Steve. Lisa looked like a pile of clothing that had been kicked around some. "Lisa?" He said carefully, knowing it was her, but somehow hoping he was making a mistake. They were her clothes but the formerly glowing and happy young face and confident and beautiful figure that once filled them was just about unrecognizable. She wasn't the same person he had played Gin Rummy with the night before. She wasn't the loving and caring mother of his son's unborn child, her glowing blue eyes had lost whatever happiness was left in her. Something horrible had occurred.

"My baby!" Lisa exclaimed, between deep and pained sobs. Frank helped her to her feet.

"The baby will be fine, Lisa. We need to get you to the clinic to see the doc. Can you walk okay?" He asked, sounding more caring and understanding than Lisa had known him to be. Little did she know that he was shocked half to death but trying to be strong for her.

"My ankle..." Lisa replied, the sobs growing worse. "He...he kicked me. He knocked me down and kicked me and stomped on my ankle."

"Who did this, Lisa? Did you know him?"

"I don't know. I don't know why he did this. I didn't know him, I didn't do anything and he knocked me down and kicked me. I told him I was pregnant and he just kept going." Lisa coughed and blood drizzled out her mouth as she leaned forward, looking like she wanted to throw up.

"Don't try to talk too much, Lisa. Save your strength, we'll call the police after we see the doctor. Come on. Lean on me. It isn't far," Frank told Lisa, trying in some way to comfort her, knowing what the blood could well mean. With a great deal of difficulty, he got Lisa to the clinic which had long since finished its business for the day, then called the doctor from a nearby pay phone to come and meet them. His head was spinning as he nearly went mad not knowing what to do or what to say. With a shaking voice, he called his wife.

"Hello?" Mrs. Hansen answered.

"Ruth honey, I found Lisa. Can you call Smitty's place and try and see if you can catch the boys and get them to meet us down at the clinic?"

"The clinic? What happened?" came the shocked reply.

"I can't say much now but Lisa got beat up. I think it could be serious. Just call the boys. Prepare them but don't tell them too much. I have to go now." Frank hung up the phone without waiting for a response, still feeling completely devastated at what had happened. He went to Lisa to see if he could get her anything. She was still crying and in pain and he was helpless to do anything.

"Where does it hurt, Lisa? Show me where he hit you." He said to her, hoping against hope not to see what he knew was most likely. She lifted her shirt and sweater up and there it was – a rupture mark on her rounded belly. She had been kicked there and kicked hard.

"He was some kind of maniac!" She gasped out between sobs. "He tried to pick me up but I told him about the baby and he just went nuts. He seemed like a freak but I never thought...I didn't..." Once again her words gave way to sobs of pain, but not the physical pain she was experiencing, the worse pain that a young mother feels knowing she was in grave danger of losing her child.

Within a short while, the doctor's car came screeching up. He didn't bother to unlock the clinic. He just took a quick look at Lisa, touched her stomach, pressed a few key points on her, then after seeing her wince in pain with each touch, he got Frank to help her into his car and, together, they sped off to the small local airport with Frank driving. The Doctor was busy calling up the Medevac Pilot and his nurse, and demanding they drop everything and get to the airport immediately. All the doctor could think of was that, if he could get her to Vancouver General in time, there might be a chance. Two lives were at stake and as Frank drove them towards the airport the Doctor's lithe German sports car navigated the curving and changing streets with the fury and skill of a panther.

When they got to the Walker Lake airport about three miles outside town, Lisa was coughing up blood again, a sickly looking black and mucous laden blood that made the doctor lose another iota of the little hope he had left for at least one of the lives that were in his caring hands. These were the worst times to be a doctor he thought, when you know the person who is hurting, when you have known them forever and they are so deathly damaged there is nothing you can do. Either way, should the baby make it or not, Lisa would need surgery that he wasn't equipped to perform to save her life, which was flowing out of her. It was a solemn ride, Frank talking a little to soothe Lisa and the odd fit of coughing and gurgling the only sounds to be heard in the car.

Within 25 minutes, a small twin-engine four seat aircraft that was kept on standby for medical evacuations was prepped by removing the rear seats to fit a gurney and the doctor's nurse who came from her home to meet them with supplies she had grabbed and started Lisa on an IV drip, though pain killers were too much of a risk at that point. Lisa was fully aware of what was happening around her and couldn't hold back her moans of pain and gasps of sorrow. Within another 10 minutes, the plane took off and headed hell bent for the Vancouver airport.

As there was no room in the plane left and no one else to tell his son the information needed, Frank stayed behind, arranging to borrow the doctor's car to return to the clinic and tell his son the many things he didn't know and the inescapable truth of what he did know, and then get his grieving son to Vancouver as fast as he could.

Frank drove back into to town with a thousand things running through his mind as he pushed the car to its limits around each bend and down each straightaway, wanting to get to the clinic as fast as he could, yet not wanting to get there at all. Would Lisa be okay? Was there any chance the baby could survive? Who was this psychopath who had done this and how could he do such a thing to a sweet girl like her? He wondered, what would this do to Steve, his son, the son he loved dearly but had such a hard time relating to, had such a hard time trying to reach. He knew the boy had a sensitive side and that he deeply loved his fiancé and had a lot of hopes and dreams for his unborn child. This will devastate him, thought Frank, even if things turn out okay. When he arrived at the clinic in town, Smitty, Colin and Steve were there waiting, standing near the spot where Lisa had earlier been sitting.

"Dad? What's going on?" Steve asked, sounding a bit angry and more than a little quizzical. "There's blood on the sidewalk! Where is Lisa and why have you got Dr. Henderson's car?"

"Take a deep breath, Stevie. There's no easy way to say this..." Frank was getting a little choked up, not wanting to say what he had to. "Someone beat up Lisa pretty bad. The doc went with her on the medical evacuation plane to Vancouver. Let's all just get in the car and get on the highway. We need to be strong for Lisa and get down to Vancouver as soon as we can."

"What?! You mean some bastard did something to..." Then it hit him and, all at once, it was like the air, the very essence had been sucked out of him. All at once, his whole history with

Lisa went past his eyes. How she used to giggle and make jokes in junior high, how he started to have a crush on her in grade ten but never told her. He saw her body develop and how it gave him more reasons to have a crush on her. Then, the amazing time at a party when both of them were a little drunk and they danced slow together and then necked in the back yard for an hour. It was so hard for him to face her the next Monday but he did and the whole relationship started from there. He became so close to her, so happy to know she loved him back. When he thought about what had happened before he got there, his face dropped and his fear and anger nearly caused him to be sick. "She's not going to…the baby. Is the baby going to be okay?"

"There's no way to tell, Stevie. Just get in the car. I think I better drive. We'll call your mother as soon as we can. Let's just get going." Steve fell silent and got in the passenger seat. His father's words made sense to him but very little else did. The concept that his true love was in danger and the fact that he was helpless to do anything about it ate away at his stomach like rat poison. He blamed himself, for being gone when she needed help the most. Tension in the car was at a boiling point as Steve sat running every negative possibility of a possible million scenarios and gritted his teeth. Even Colin knew he needed to sit without noise or interference at that terrible time. All the poor kid understood was that something bad had happened and anything he could say or do could take the lid off the pressure cooker and direct the blast at himself. He did and said nothing as he had done so many times before when adult stuff was going on.

It was normally a four hour drive or a one hour plane trip to downtown Vancouver from Walker Lake but the plane carrying Lisa landed 40 minutes after it took off and, soon after, an ambulance rushed Lisa to Vancouver General, arriving in another 22 minutes. The Hansen men and Smitty arrived two hours later. They played no music: they didn't talk and Frank kept the finely tuned German automobile going at nearly redline the whole way, weaving in and out of traffic at speeds over 160km/hr. When they arrived at the front doors of the hospital, they were all wound up tighter than any of them cared to be.

They walked up to the main information desk and were directed where to go and wait. When they got there, Frank and Steve walked up to the surgery ward nurse.

"Hello, miss. I was wondering if I could get some information...," Steve's father asked, somewhat overly politely.

"Sir, I will have to ask you to sit down and wait. We have two serious cases going on here. The doctor will come out and call you when he can." Frank felt insulted and wanted to lash out at her, but all he could do was sit and say what he could, do what he could, to keep his son on an even keel.

"Hey that's my fiancée in there!" Steve yelled as Frank tried to hold him back. A look of surprise came over the desk nurse's face, and she seemed to turn into a kind person in just seconds.

"I'm sorry, Sir. I'm deeply sorry, but we don't know anything right now. I promise I will tell you what we know as soon as we know anything. It just won't help to disturb the Doctors right now."

Despite the boiling pressure of his emotions, Frank knew it wouldn't help at all if he got angry himself, even though he felt some kind of masculine obligation to do so. If he was a boiling pressure cooker, his son had to be a burning powder keg. Steve was the kind of person who would do anything for his family members. There was even a time when his little brother Colin was being bullied at his school and Steve went and watched the playground and caught up with the kid on his way home. He didn't hit him but he sure did scare him and Colin kept having fewer and fewer bullies from then on, especially since Steve took it upon himself to teach Colin the right way to deal with that sort of thing.

After 20 minutes or so of nervous pacing and few words, an orderly pushed out a gurney from the surgery area with the face covered up. Steve yelled out "Lisa!" and bolted over to intercept the gurney, hoping to catch one last glimpse of the love of his life. He pulled back the sheet and it wasn't Lisa: it was an elderly woman. The sight shocked him a bit but the idea that it wasn't Lisa gave him some comfort. The orderly looked like he was going to belt him but held back, knowing that this kind of sight of a person on a gurney covered up can be extremely disturbing. Steve apologized profusely, and after a stern warning from the nurse, he sat down, scared at what he had seen, but relieved at least for the moment. It was much like the feeling a gambler might have when he makes a stupid move and leaves himself open to an easy loss, then watches as the blackjack dealer breaks 21. There was still a chance but only more chances to gamble. It wasn't a good feeling.

Once again, now that the nurse at the desk seemed to have time, the senior Hansen family member went up to talk to her and she was much kinder this time. She made a phone call and soon their Dr. Henderson and the nurse from Walker Lake came to see them. Frank and Steve couldn't seem to stop from asking the two question after question even though they understood very little from what answers the medical professionals could give. What the doctor was trying to avoid saying but, eventually couldn't avoid, was that there was really no chance for the baby to live. With one of the kicks she had received, Lisa's womb had ruptured and as a result her water had broken in the airplane, not to mention that unknown damage had resulted from the other kicks. The fetus was just too young to survive for the time it took to get there, not to mention Lisa's weakened condition.

After four more hours of waiting, pacing, asking questions that they knew the inevitable answers to, a middle aged surgeon with graying hair and strained but intelligent and caring looking green eyes came in to speak to them, with more than a little blood on his scrubs. He took off his mask, introduced himself only as John, not doctor or any other title. Before he said much, he went down on one knee to match young Colin's height and spoke to him as only a man experienced in fathering could, then gave him a dollar coin to go get a candy bar from a machine down the hall.

"Is the husband here?" the surgeon asked, looking towards Steve and Smitty.

"Fiancé, actually. I'm Steve Hansen. This is my dad, Frank, and a family friend, Smitty," Steve said, offering his hand. Even in this terrible moment, Steve's Dad looked on Steve with a great sense of pride in the strength and maturity he showed. The specialist slipped off a glove and shook Steve's hand. "And I guess you know our home town doctor and nurse here."

"Yes, I do. Steve, I have some bad news and good news. The good news is we stabilized Lisa's condition. I think you have been told there was just no way to help your unborn child." The surgeon felt a wave of compassion as he saw the young man's eyes get glassy though he held back full tears.

"I understand. What's this about bad news? Isn't it bad enough we lost our child?" Steve was trying to stay strong but his voice faltered a bit as he asked.

"Well, all I can really say is that with the damage your fiancée received from her beating, she is going to be recovering for a while, and she may need more treatment and possibly more surgery after we know more. I've done everything I can, but this person that did this thing to her was quite brutal." With the words the surgeon uttered, Steve felt a black and sinking feeling from his upper chest to the pit of his stomach. Revenge was the only word he could think of.

He wanted to ball his fists, scream and punch a hole in the wall but he kept his cool with some difficulty. "And, one other thing. When Lisa gets to feel a bit better, we want her to talk to the police. This person is violent. I'm hoping you will cooperate, too. Do you have a place here in the city you can stay for a few days or more?"

"I know a hotel over on Main Street that I use when I'm in town," Steve replied, through his gritted teeth, as he avoided looking into the kind eyes of the man speaking to him.

"Just leave the number with the duty nurse at the desk there and we'll contact you. Right now, your fiancée needs rest and I think you do, too. I don't recommend you go through this alone. Can your friend Smitty here stay in town with you until we can release Lisa?"

"Yes, sir, I can." Smitty said, then turned to Steve. "I'm not going to let you stay in that run-down place near the train station. Those ancient hotels may only charge twenty bucks a night but you have to share a shower and your room with mice and cockroaches. I'm pretty sure I can get my dad to set us up in a hotel he stays at that's much better and cleaner than that."

"I think that's a great idea. Be easy on yourself, the best thing you can do right now is to treat yourself well. Get a good night's sleep and let's be thankful things aren't worse," the surgeon concluded, then put a hand on Steve's shoulder and guided him out of the waiting room in silence. As they walked off, Steve's nose began to run and the beginnings of more tears welled up in his eyes. All he could feel, if he had the words to describe it, was deadness inside.

Chapter Four

After a few phone calls and a brief talk, the two young men got into Doctor Henderson's car and not far into their trip, Smitty could see that his best friend was both crying and praying as he sat in the back seat alone.

Doctor Henderson dropped them off, wishing he knew more to say to the boys. He hoped that they weren't going to do anything to hurt themselves or Lisa's attacker. However, he also knew that, often despite all efforts to the contrary, this was what young men were taught was the right thing to do. Under his breath, Dr. Henderson cursed the fact that kids in this country were brought up on television and movie violence.

When the doctor left them at the hotel to return and pick up Frank and Colin and bring them home to Walker Lake all he could think to say to them was, "'Watch him, Smitty. It's all in God's hands now. Don't forget that Lisa is still going to need you two to be strong."

"Thanks, Doc. I'll do my best," Smitty replied.

As he pulled away, Dr. Henderson wondered if anyone's best could be enough.

The two young men went inside the large and well-kept hotel and checked into a double room. They solemnly rode up the elevator and walked down the hall to the small chamber where they most likely would be spending a sleepless night. Smitty really wanted to say the right things to Steve, but he had never experienced anything so horrible, so gut-wrenchingly painful. Steve sat down on one of the beds and it was as if there was a storm cloud over his head.

Smitty had never seen Steve so serious and stuck inside his own thoughts. For a moment he thought back to when they were in junior high and Steve had slipped on some rocks and hit his head. He got up, trying always to be the tough guy and walked on the trail they were hiking. Little did he know he had a concussion and could have died. A mile or so down the road, Steve started throwing up and complained of being dizzy and he still didn't seem to think he needed help. Smitty ended up half-carrying him to the highway. Even years later, Steve didn't like to talk about the time he needed help because he had a concussion.

Steve stood up, breaking Smitty's concentration. He looked as though an idea had come to him and said, without even looking at his best friend, "I'm going to go out and get a toothbrush."

As he opened the door, Smitty darted up and pushed the door shut and said, "I'll go with you, Steve. This isn't Main Street but there are a lot of characters in this city this time of night." It was nearing two a.m. and they weren't in a small town, but a city of 1.3 million.

"I saw a store just around the corner and all the streets are lighted. You stay here and try to get some room service. I could use a good burger and fries. I need a snack and clean teeth before I can sleep right now," Steve replied in something of a flat monotone that implied he had no intentions of doing such things.

"Alright, Stevie, you're not a kid anymore. I think I know what you want to do. That store we saw was a liquor store. Go and get a bottle and get a few beers for me. A drink or two might help us get through this, and let us sleep a bit, no matter what the doc suggested," Smitty declared.

"Yeah, okay. I'll be right back, but I meant what I said: I'm hungry. Get us some cheeseburgers, if you can."

In a few minutes, Steve returned with a 750 ml bottle of whiskey and a six-pack of American beer for his buddy. He pulled a beer off the plastic six-pack holder and handed one over. Then, he asked, "Want any rye with that?" After Smitty shook his head, indicating no, Steve unscrewed the top of the bottle, broke the seal and drank right out of it, tipping it back far to take in as much of the flammable liquid as he could.

"Whoa. Good stuff." Steve's voice croaked as his face grew flushed. He laid back on his bed and watched as Smitty downed his first beer.

They hadn't done this much, but they had done it enough to know they were going to get so drunk they would be throwing up and regretting it within a few short hours. But, for the time being, they were going to feel good or at least, feel no pain. It didn't take long for the liquor to start to take effect on Steve. He liked his whiskey; it made him feel like John Wayne about to go rescue a damsel in distress. The waves of pleasure that went through him as he drank made him feel better than he had been feeling for some time.

"What's all going through your head, dude?" Smitty asked, a little apprehensively.

"I'm just thinking. Wondering who would do this. Why they would do this? Why she..." Steve choked on a tear as he spoke, and tried to wash it away with another swig of booze, which made him cough. "You know, Smitty, she was the first girl I ever...you know. For a long time, I saw all the other guys talking about their girlfriends and I just thought I was too ugly or too shy or too poor to ever have one. Then, Lisa came along and the whole sex thing didn't matter anymore. We connected, we liked all the same music and stuff. It was like we were made for each other. Then, finally the sex did come and all I could think about was how much it turned me on that I was going to get this awesome, wonderful young woman pregnant and I was going to get a chance to have a whole life to father and to guide. I had Colin, but that wasn't really the same. I just can't describe it. It was like we fell in love, and then, we were crazy mad attracted to each other, and so we did it, and then, a whole new life came about because of our love. Now, that's all destroyed."

"Things are going to be okay, man," Smitty said, as he leaned over and patted Steve on the back. "Look on the bright side: a lot of women have miscarriages, I learned this in biology... you two can have another one. Trust me: things will work out. And, let me tell you something about all those other guys you mentioned. They were all full of shit: none of them were really having any sex, except the odd drunk guy who didn't remember things the next day, anyhow. What they had was five minutes to get off. What you and Lisa have can be forever."

"But, who in our town would do something like this?" Steve said, changing the subject of the conversation as he took a smaller sip of his whiskey, and the anguish in his face and voice became more apparent. "There's only one thing I think is possible."

"What's that, man-o?" Smitty replied.

"Well, a while back, I'm not sure why I even remember this, maybe because it made me kind of wonder about Lisa — she said she used to have this boyfriend and he was a really bad dude but she liked that shit. Being bad. I've heard about that... you know, women who like the bad boys and all that. Made me kind of wonder for a while if she loved me. You know, when I was younger, I would talk to my mom about all this, and I made a decision that no matter what, I wasn't going to be a guy like that. Hell, I practically raised Colin. I never bullied or shunned him. But, all the time, I see women going with these assholes. Hey-remember that guy, Dan West? Man, I would like to take a round out of him. Can you imagine a guy pumping steroids in grade nine? Pumping steroids, bullying everyone, still got the best looking women. I hope his testicles shrunk from all that stuff. But something tells me these fuck-heads get away with all that."

"Steve, man, the cops will find this guy. Don't let it take over your brain. She probably knows who did it and just wants to feel safe before she talks. Some of these guys keep long grudges. She probably realized what a jerk he was and dumped him cold and he couldn't take it. Just let her get to feel better and things will go your way."

"Smitty, my friend, I really don't know how I could go through all this without you, man... I..." Steve had a hard time getting the words out as he started to get choked up again. Smitty came towards him and hugged Steve as he started to sob a bit before saying, "I just love her so much. I can't understand any of this. If the cops can't find this guy, or if he gets off, or gets a light sentence..."

"What can you do, bud? You're just a good-hearted, small town dude. This guy is some psycho asshole and he might even have connections," Smitty said, taking Steve by the shoulders and looking at his tear-stained face.

Steve took another long pull on the whiskey, wiped away the tears, as his facial appearance grew more somber, then he spoke. "Well, I have been thinking about something. You remember Yuri?" he asked Smitty.

"Yuri...Yuri...Oh yeah, that Russian guy who came here when we were in grade nine. Nice guy. What brings that up?" Smitty replied, not knowing where this was going, but not liking what he guessed about it.

"Did you ever meet a tougher guy than him?" Steve probed.

"No, not that I know of. He took all that martial arts stuff pretty serious, plus what was his old man — Spetznatz? Those Russian Special Forces Airborne guys. He must have used to get the shit kicked out of him by his old man. Remember how he would come to school with all those bruises — and those scars we saw on him changing in gym. You going to pay him to get revenge?" Smitty replied.

"Better," Steve answered, pausing to sip more booze. "I'm going to get him to train me and help me plan something. I think he will too, he would help anyone. Remember when Dan West called a commie and the next day Dan came to school with two black eyes and a better attitude? Maybe his dad will even help. His dad took care of that dude who was poisoning dogs that one time, remember?"

"Remember? Ha! He practically pulled the guy's nose off his face. The poor bastard had to move out of town because everyone knew who he was and what he did. Crazy bastard, that old guy! Do you realize what you would be getting into, though? You'd be up for all the same beatings Yuri took. Let the cops take care of this dude," Smitty replied, still trying not swear or glorify what was going to happen, but feeling his morals slip away as he opened and sipped at his third beer. "What is it you're figuring on doing? And, if you do, how do you think for a minute you could get away with it?"

"That's two questions," Steve said, raising a finger on his bottle hand, now well on his way to feeling no pain. "To the first question, what am I going to do? I say, that little son of a bitch not only killed my child and beat Lisa near to death. I have been thinking that since he did this for me I should return the favor. As for your second question, I don't really give a fuck. I can't live in that town forever knowing the guy who killed my baby was free to roam and do what he wants. If the cops get him, fine. But, like I said, if he goes scott free or gets a light sentence, I'm going to take things into my own hands."

This was maybe the third or fourth time Smitty had heard his friend swear. Looking at his face, and the dead serious look in his eyes, he knew Steve was headed down a dark and dangerous path that he didn't want to come along down. All he could think of was to say the words, "Steve, you do realize this is like you were headed down Green Mountain Road in a tractor trailer hauling twenty tons of shit on black ice?"

"Yeah, what's it to you?"

"How can I help?"

The two young men talked of their plans a little further, and then passed out for a few hours of restless sleep. Steve dreamed of an incredibly vivid sexual experience with Lisa who somehow turned into a young woman from school who he had once had a crush on. Both parts of the dream felt good, and he didn't want the dream to end, but somehow he knew he would most likely have neither woman, or so his unconscious mind had told him. When they woke up, Steve went and bought a bottle of cola from one of the hotel's vending machines, and poured half of it out in the hotel room sink, then added what was left of his whiskey from the night before. He had no intention of facing the pain he was going through in a sober condition, despite what anyone may have told him. When that was done, they checked out, not bothering to shower, only taking time to ask Steve's dad to take a day off work and bring them a change of clothes and a few things that Lisa may need. When Steve called him, his dad knew he had been drinking but said nothing. Little did Steve realize, that his dad was going through just about as much torment as he was.

The two made their way to the hospital and were allowed to briefly talk with Lisa as she lay in her bed, all bruised and battered, but still happy to see them.

"Steve, I'm so sorry," was the first thing she said, as she was making a huge effort to hold back her emotions from them. Lisa felt so much guilt, remorse, and physical pain though that her underlying fears were highly visible to Steve and Smitty.

"What do you have to be sorry about?" He replied, betraying almost a state of anger towards Lisa for blaming herself.

"If I hadn't gone out with that jerk in the first place, this wouldn't have happened," Lisa said, giving a bit of a sniffle and trying hard to look away to hide her tears.

"Whatever may have happened between him and you, didn't give him any right to do what he did. And, believe me, there is going to be hell to pay for this," Steve said, now displaying what he felt was righteous anger in his voice.

"You can't... you just can't Steve," Lisa said, reaching out her hand through the pain to touch the hand of the young man she loved dearly. "He knows people around town. He can do more than you think...some of the things he used to get into...I can hardly believe I even went out with him at all. I didn't even really want to. It was all one-sided." Lisa sobbed when she said this, partially from physical pain, largely from emotional.

As though all things were timed by the hand of God, just as Lisa began to cry, a young nurse came in as though she had heard the conversation and told the Steve and Lisa that the police had come down from Walker Lake and were there to talk with them. Steve and Smitty went outside of Lisa's room to see the RCMP sergeant of the local detachment from their hometown and another constable. They looked quite solemn and serious.

"Mr. Hansen, Mr. Smith," Sergeant Jonsonsaid, acknowledging them. "We have a few questions to ask you about this unfortunate mess. It won't take too long, but we have to do it so we can make sure justice is done."

"We don't know a whole lot, except that it was her ex-boyfriend Sean Davie. He's the one you're after," Smitty said, knowing that talking to these officers would be extremely difficult for Steve to do at that time.

"Did you witness this happen?" The sergeant asked, seeming a little disappointed.

"No, Mr. Hansen. Steve's dad, first found her downtown and took her into the clinic. Lisa in there can identify the guy," Smitty said, seeming a little confused.

"Yes, well uh..." The sergeant replied, sounding a little hesitant. "We spoke to Steve's dad and he didn't seem to have any direct knowledge of the crime either. You see, when Lisa's doctor called we gathered that it was this Sean character. He's been on our radar for some time, and we went and checked him out. We searched his room at home. We talked to him for quite a while and we couldn't even come up with enough to hold him. He had an alibi, and we found no blood on any of his clothes, or any other evidence, for that matter."

"What the hell do you mean?" Steve said angrily. "That asshole beat her up so bad she can never have kids...we can never have kids. Are you saying you're not even going to arrest him?"

"Unfortunately that's exactly what I'm saying, and I'll thank you to show a little respect. This case has us pretty upset...I would even say pissed off. We don't like this kind of thing around Walker Lake, but this kid covered his bases. All it comes down to is one witness against another. I want you to know that you have a right to protect your family members, but I also want to tell you if you go on some little vigilante justice mission and I find out about it, I WILL charge you.

"Are you saying you're going to protect this piece of garbage?"

"That's exactly what I'm saying," the senior constable answered. "I don't like it much when people can laugh at the law, especially in the same town I have two young daughters in. I can't help you any further than gathering evidence and laying charges. I just want to advise you to walk very carefully and try hard to keep your nose clean enough I don't end up having to come along and wipe it for you."

"Thanks, Officer, but I don't think we'll take you up on that offer," Smitty said to the sergeant, putting his arm in front of Steve just in case, and leading him away from the cop. Smitty did this knowing full well what his friend had talked about so adamantly the night before was just exactly what this officer was suggesting he not do.

For the rest of the day, Steve and Smitty sat in a waiting area in the recovery ward Lisa was on, going in to talk with her when she was rested and could face them for a few minutes. Smitty started getting extremely bored as Steve wasn't talking much and the magazines left sitting were mostly for women. He wanted to be there for his friend, who he had never seen so depressed or so determined to stay drunk. Maybe it was because then he wouldn't feel anything, and wouldn't have the need to fly into a rage at the smallest thing, which it had seemed he was capable of doing at times.

Later in the day, Smitty's dad came down and gave him a credit card, so they could rent a car to get around in and get a decent hotel room. He could tell that the boys had been drinking. The smell was obvious, which he didn't like much, but at such a time, Mr. Smith didn't really know what to say or do. Over the years of friendship, Mr. Smith had come to know Steve just about as well as if he were one of his own boys. It hurt him deeply to see both of them messed up bad enough to want to do such a thing to themselves, not to mention the effect it had on the people around them. All he really knew to do was to give them a few words of encouragement and try to make sure they didn't want for anything. As he drove home in his own car, he said a silent prayer for the three of them, asking Jesus to help them through what people that age should never have to go through.

Chapter Five

Despite Steve's cravings and frustration, that night, the two men didn't pick up any booze before going to sleep. Lisa had let on that she knew he was drinking and wasn't happy about it, and Steve in no way wanted to make any of this harder on her. In the dark, just like they used to do when they were out camping or on sleepovers, Steve and Smitty were able to talk to each other more openly and honestly than at any other time. It seemed somehow that over the years as they were friends, they were always either talking about girls or about getting older. For awhile, as they ignored the sounds of the streets, Steve talked for a long time about all the things he loved about Lisa.

Smitty tried to explain to him, as his own dad had once explained, that underneath the good looks and the big boobs, there was a lot to love about a woman. After that, with some thought and exchange of personal philosophies, Steve told his buddy that he was swearing off any more intoxicants until "things were taken care of." That his good friend chose those words brought concern to Smitty. He didn't know if Steve meant he was going to go ballistic on booze when this set goal was accomplished, and he didn't really know what "taken care of" meant, but he had a good idea. He was embarrassed about it, but Smitty had a deep faith within him that his father had impressed on him and he tried to explain how violence only begets violence and how the Bible clearly stated that people weren't meant to get personal revenge.

In reply, Steve impressed Smitty at first by saying he had read the small Gideon Bible they had both gotten in school years ago and his favorite passage was in Proverbs. "A loving doe, a graceful deer, may her breasts satisfy you at all times." It was funny, and Smitty knew it really was in the Bible, but part of him really wanted Steve to understand God's word. After what had happened, and how it seemed to affect Steve, Smitty was getting worried about the path his friend was headed down.

Was his best friend going to kill this Sean character, or torture him? And how far would things go? Would his retaliations be met with more retaliations and escalations? Although they had known each other for such a long time, Smitty wondered to himself what Steve might be capable of. Heaven knows, he thought, what would he himself be capable of, and what would he get dragged into if this turned into a small Walker Lake war?

Steve had a pretty hard time getting to sleep, tossing and turning, trying to find the position but he couldn't seem to lay still in any of them. Finally, he drifted off and soon he slipped into a dream of Walker Lake, hiking up a mountain and getting to a high altitude and looking out over a range of mountains as the sun rose behind them. It seemed that the gates of heaven had opened up. Although he needed his binoculars to see, he could see an image of Jesus Christ on a cross, bleeding, his wounds somehow feeding off Steve's boiling hate and anger. As he stood watching, he also saw his family and friends, schoolmates and teachers, one by one, being taken away, up towards the perfect white light about Jesus. But Steve remained, full of anger and hate and the hurt from it was intense. Steve woke up with a start. He made a mental point not to sleep without booze anymore. It was so much easier that way.

In the morning, Steve got up first and took the car keys, and was gone until after Smitty woke up. When he returned, he was sweaty and looking exhausted. He had been using few words, but felt he owed an explanation, so Steve said to his best friend, "Woke up early, went for a jog around Stanley Park. Only made it about four miles. I need to tune myself up." By the tone in his voice and the look on his face, Smitty could tell that not only Steve's legs, but his whole being was hurting. It was more than likely that Steve had gone on this jaunt to punish himself, as a sort of penance despite that they weren't Catholic. It was also more than likely that Steve had pushed himself so far with a combined desire to punish Sean, who was going to become the mantra Steve would use to get himself through this painful time.

After as healthy a breakfast as they could get without spending $40.00 in the hotel restaurant for it, the two young men made their way to the hospital. When they arrived, they didn't have to wait long to talk with Lisa's Doctor who called himself just John as before.

"Good morning gentleman. I was hoping I could find you here. I have some good news, finally. Lisa is doing quite well, despite the surgery and problems, and as long as you can assure me someone will be around to take care of her, I think in about three more days you can take her home. I have to stress though, that she has really been through quite a bit and is feeling very depressed. With her condition I don't really want to give her anything for mood, but when she is feeling better if things persist, I am going to give instructions to your family doctor to give her a prescription of a drug we call fluoxetine."

"What kind of prescription is that?" Steve asked.

"It is an anti-depressant we have found to be quite effective, especially with women who have gone through the hormonal changes that follows pregnancy. I am hoping she will be fine after we can get her to some counseling, but we need to keep a close eye on how she is doing, so I want to see her for a follow up in about two weeks, then again in a month. She will need to come here to the hospital," the doctor asked him in reply.

"There should be no problem. But as for this counseling, where can we go for that?" Steve asked.

"We should be able to set you up with something in Walker Lake, give it about a week after you get home and try not to get too stressed out about anything. It would be best if you both could go to the sessions: they can be very beneficial." As the doctor said the word 'beneficial,' seemingly on cue, there was a series of beeps coming from his belt pager. He took the pager in his hand and looked at it, made a bit of a face, then apologized to Steve and excused himself.

Within a few minutes, an observant nurse could see they were waiting and told Stevie and Smitty that they could visit Lisa.

"Hey, girl." Steve said to Lisa, as she lay with her blackened eyes closed. When her eyes opened, Steve felt a bit of anticipation, knowing that Lisa had such pretty eyes, but when she opened them the whites of her eyes had blood marks in them from broken vessels, and he returned in short order to his angry state of mind, which he concealed from her. "We're going to take you home soon, baby." He wished he hadn't used the pet name 'baby,' but it just kind of slipped off his tongue. They had been calling each other that for years.

"Back to Walker Lake?" Lisa queried.

"Back to the Lake. Unless you have some better place to go," Steve replied.

"I don't know if I want to go back there-even if that jerk who did this is in jail," Lisa answered.

Steve and Smitty looked at each other, not knowing what to say. It was Smitty who spoke first. "We talked to the cops, Lisa. They said they couldn't even charge him. They couldn't find any evidence other than your statement versus his statement.

We're going to help you, though...." He decided to stop himself from saying any more from that point.

"They can't charge him? What am I going to do? What if he comes after us again? What if he decides to keep me quiet for good?" Lisa said somewhat frantically, though her words showed more sense it seemed, than Steve's.

"I promise you girl. We're going to take care of things. We have things worked out. We just can't talk about it too much," Steve offered.

"You're going to beat him up? Then what happens? He comes back with a baseball bat or an axe or a gun? No way. My parents are coming down. I'm going to ask them for money to get an apartment here in the city by myself. I love you, Stevie, but I can't go back to Walker Lake, not while that animal is free. Do what you will, but if you go to jail, don't expect me to wait for you. I want to get married, but I don't need a man who cares more about revenge than he does about me. I'm going to live here for a while. If you can really sort things out or not, I don't want to go back. I'm sick of the small town garbage. I can't trust anyone to keep a secret or forgive even the smallest transgression. I can't even think for myself, and I'm almost twenty-one."

"Where did all this come from? You can't trust me? You don't believe I can keep you safe? Someone is filling you full of crap," Steve said, both hurt and angered at the whole situation.

"I spoke to their counselor here after you left. We talked for quite a while. She was saying I have a few issues to work on, and I think I'm going to have a few sessions, work on a few of those issues, get things out, then in a month or two, if you still want me and things are going better, you can come and live here with me," Lisa answered, standing up to someone perhaps for the first time ever.

"If that's what you want, I'm behind you. Will you call me, at least?" Steve said, a bit sheepishly.

"Of course I will. I'll probably call you every day. Nothing has changed, but that I think I will be a lot better off here, where I can get some help and feel a bit better and safer about things," Lisa replied to Steve, sounding more caring in this last exchange of words.

"Then far be it from me to stand in your way, beautiful." He leaned over and brushed her soft and silky hair away from her forehead and kissed it gently, not wanting to cause her more pain than necessary.

Steve and Smitty left to find a nearby liquor store for a mickey of vodka, since vodka when properly made gives off no odor. He then bought a large bottle of water, which he poured out and replaced with the booze. He liked how the vodka tasted and how when it went down, it seemed to go right to his head. It gave him confidence and a feeling of taking a holiday from reality. In a way, he wished he had started drinking a long time ago. It didn't bother him that in this section of Vancouver there was a large string of cheap hotels with bars in them full of people who met their match in a bottle just like he had.

Over the next few days, Steve went for more jogs, and visited Lisa as much as he could. After a bit of arguing and a lot of urging, he convinced Smitty that he was okay on his own. And so finally, after 11 days, Smitty left for Walker Lake. Steve helped arrange things so that there was a home care nurse available to stay with Lisa when she was ready to leave the hospital. He moved into a run-down old hotel on Main Street that had been built in the days when the railroad was king and likely had the same cockroaches and piss stains in the hallways as it did back then. It was near the main transit station though, so he could get just about everywhere in Vancouver without a car. Steve also picked himself up a used bike and managed to wrangle a cheap membership at a local recreation centre and spent as much of his time in one form of physical activity or another, as he could, pushing himself harder and harder, filling his head with images of anger and retribution, driving himself further each day, each workout.

His days began early. He began with a ritual of getting suited up in a cheap set of sweats and an expensive pair of running shoes and headed off to run the circumference of Stanley Park. It was a long jog – nearly ten miles — and, for the first while, he had to walk part of it or stop to rest. But with each day, he went further and further without stopping. It was a cleansing to him, leaving the poor and downtrodden area he had his room in, going past the ships moored in the waterways, puffing steamy clouds of breath as he started out in the park with a view of the incredible scenery of the North Shore, always with his heart pumping hard and all the toxins and frustrations working their way out in the open through the pain and the sweat. He would hit his rhythm as he jogged under the massive Lions Gate Bridge, going on and on, sometimes for what seemed like hours, as he pushed himself and rounded the edge of the park with a view of the open water that lay between Vancouver and Vancouver Island. It was here that he felt most at home, there were often other runners and cyclists on the trail, but at this far point he was almost always alone and able to experience the runner's high which made the scenery even more incredible to witness. Then a sense of sadness would come to him as he ran past Siwash Rock and the plaque that was made to honor the memory of a young boy who broke his neck diving off of it. The sadness was not so much for the boy, but for the whole concept that this tall rock marked his return to the city, to the pain, the hunger, the poverty, the traffic, the smog, the rudeness that every former resident of a small town noticed quickly in a city of this size, beautiful as it was. It was everything he hated about life away from Walker Lake, but wanted to gain victory over of, because of his love for Lisa. He returned to the city each time a little stronger, a little more ready to put his whole plan into action, but he never finished a workout any happier.

When Steve returned to his hotel, he would shower in the one bathroom afforded each floor of the hotel, change, and then eat a leisurely breakfast of eggs, bacon, toast with honey, orange juice and milk at a nearby restaurant. It sounded like a lot of calories, and it was, but he had burned a lot in the almost two hours of running he did each day, added with a regimen of strength exercises and bicycle riding that he would also put himself through, at other times of the day. After his meal, he would take a short nap and then get his mickey of vodka for the day, disguise it in a water bottle, and sip away at it or even go into a restaurant and add it to a glass of orange juice and let himself get just a little bit numb before he faced anyone or anything outside of Stanley Park. Though he was a morning drinker, he wouldn't drink a lot before he went to see Lisa. He wanted to moderate all of his drinking, but Steve found that after a few hours alone with himself thinking about the life he could have had before Sean came along, he had to have some kind of numbing effect to keep from going crazy.

After a few more days and a few more punishing workouts went by, Lisa's apartment was ready and she left the hotel she had been staying in for the interim. The only real bad part of Lisa getting her life in order was that Steve was now closer to having to face the concept of leaving Walker Lake, though he would be returning to it for a short while. Steve drove Lisa to the apartment her parents had helped her get, then walked his true love to her door. Steve was distant as they walked. Lisa couldn't understand Steve's dislike for Vancouver. To her, it was a beautiful place, filled with opportunities and adventures that played themselves out for the older and more mature people in the towers that marked the skyline of the great city, and the ones that were for the young on Friday and Saturday nights with nightlife like no other place this side of Ontario.

When they got to her new apartment, the two stood

at the doorway, not really knowing what to do or say. Steve was looking down, his head so filled with anger it barely had room to think about the fact that he and Lisa hadn't made love since before the incident. Lisa knew though and, taking things into her own hands, she put her hand under Steve's chin and lifted his head so he could look into her eyes. For the first time in a while, he didn't see fear or sadness: he didn't see pain. He saw the young woman he had loved dearly and deeply and who he had wanted to spend the rest of his life with. Her eyes were so moist and beautiful, her face now healed of its wounds was so sensuous, in the fullness of her lips and the upward curve of her cute little nose. "Come here, handsome." was all she had to say.

Steve stepped forward to hold her and he could feel her large breasts pressing into him. It made his penis grow erect and Lisa could tell, because she was pressing her whole body into him. Almost simultaneously, their right arms that were around each other's backs went downwards to caress each other's butts and, as they realized this, they laughed, but they didn't take their hands away. Leaning back, Steve looked right into Lisa's eyes, then moved in for a deep, tongue probing kiss. They were both so filled with passion that no words had to be said. They broke their grip for just a moment so Lisa could get out her keys, and they quickly went inside and locked the door behind themselves.

When they got inside, they barely had time to admire the work Lisa's mom had put into making this faraway apartment a home for Lisa. Not only did she put in leather sofas and a TV, but she also put fine touches in like lace curtains and oil paintings of places that reminded both of them of the home they truly loved.

They embraced again, as they got in the door and, Lisa kept her mouth locked onto Steve's as she unbuttoned her blouse to reveal she wasn't wearing a bra. This made Steve nearly explode down under as he had forgotten what an awesome body she had: those firm, round, and smooth breasts he had for so many years wanted to caress when the two of them were just close friends and he was trying to play the noble gentleman by not 'spoiling' their friendship. Now of course, those boobs were all his, and he broke the lip lock for just a moment as he moved downwards to lick and fondle her wonderful God-given beauty. He undid the top button on her jeans and unzipped to discover that she hadn't worn panties either. It was amazing for him to think that this incredible person, strong and caring, loving and giving, beautiful and intelligent, could keep herself for him, and for him only.

They made it into the bedroom, and, with more fumbling, Lisa laid back on the bed, naked and gorgeous, as her lover stood above her, stripping off his clothes. When Steve took off his shirt, Lisa grew even more moist between the thighs, just watching the rope-like muscles he had been developing over the past while. He had somehow become even more attractive to her, and, in her mind, it was the most wonderful thing in the world. Steve then stripped off his pants and underwear, and though his erection was throbbing, and he wanted desperately to climb on top of the woman he loved, he held back and went down on her, spreading the lips of her vagina and working at her with his tongue. She was already way along as it was, but these new actions brought shuddering waves of pleasure through Lisa's whole body. She hoped the walls were thick in this new place, because as she came, she couldn't hold back the powerful desire to moan so loud, she feared being arrested for disturbing the peace.

Once he had gotten all he could get Lisa to experience, Steve climbed on top of her and, reached down to guide his hardness into her. It felt so incredible to be on top of her, sliding his dick slowly in and out of her, holding back his explosion of ecstasy as long as he could, then finally blasting a months' worth of cum deep inside of her. He could have died happy at that moment, as he collapsed beside his lover and she put her arms around him, and gave him an unflinching gaze that told him he was her master and king. It was the most perfect experience of lovemaking either of them had known, but Steve wanted her to have the time and the space to recover, and maybe mature some from her time alone, so he didn't push her by asking to stay. He just got up after she had drifted off to sleep, took a shower, dressed quietly, and made his way to the bus station, where he would catch his ride back to Walker Lake, renewed, refreshed, but alone.

Chapter Six

It wasn't a very long ride on the bus back to Walker Lake; however, Steve wished it was a very long one. Looking out the window at the trees and the mountains, the cliffs and the valleys, it seemed that he could get a lot of thinking done. What if Lisa and he could adopt? What if they could try and make a fresh start and go to another small town with Smitty and start their outdoor adventure company there? It could be possible. But, the whole idea of running away didn't seem right to him. He didn't even like the idea of being in Vancouver for a short time. There had to be something he could do. He knew what he wanted to do; he just had to get up some courage to do it.

Before he could have all the thinking time he wanted, and before he could work out in his head even half the problems he faced, the bus pulled into the parking lot of the small strip mall in his home town. Steve looked out the window to see that his parents and his little brother, along with Smitty, had gathered to welcome him back. The first thing he did when he got off the bus, was to go up and hug his mother, the symbol of stability for the whole family. Then, he picked up Colin in his arms, hiked him up on his shoulder, and carried his bag in one arm and the boy in the other.

"Getting pretty fit I see, Steve," his dad said to him. "That's a good way to boil off your frustrations."

"Trying to anyhow," Steve replied.

"We have a bit of a surprise for you when you get home, Stevie!" His mom said, with a bit of excitement in her voice.

“Yeah, “ Colin said, the happiness spilling over into his voice, as well. “Poppa is building the new house!”

“Colin!!” Their mom said sternly, “You weren’t supposed to say until we got back and he could see for himself!”

“Sorry, Momma. Sorry, Stevie,“ Colin said, now sounding a little sad.

“It’s okay, baby brother. I had a pretty good idea about it anyhow. Now I can help you guys build it, at least for a while. I think you might have to rent out the trailer though: Lisa and I won’t be needing it for some time,” Steve said plainly.

“What? What’s wrong, Stevie?” His mom asked.

“Lisa wants to stay in Vancouver when she’s all done being healed. She wants me to come and stay with her down there,” Steve answered.

“Vancouver? What will you do...what will we do with you in Vancouver?” Steve’s mom questioned. Her words filled Steve with a wash of guilt at the idea of ever leaving his beloved home and his close, caring family members, including his dad who had his good days and bad days.

“That part, I haven’t got worked out yet, but I’m working on a little something that might change her mind,” Steve said.

“Change her mind? You don’t mean you’re going to try and...“ Steve’s mom tried to ask before being interrupted by his dad.

“Just let the boy do what he has to, dear. He’s getting a little old for us to stand in his way.”

“Just be careful, Stevie. And try and do the right thing, for me. Would you?” His mom pleaded.

“I can do that Mom, I can do that,” Steve said, as he looked off into the distance, a bit glassy eyed and took his water bottle out for a sip. This time he felt as though he didn’t really need it, so after just a sip he tossed it in a nearby garbage can. Then, they all got into the Hansen family truck in silence, and drove off to Green Mountain Road and home. Somehow for Steve, everything had changed. Everything seemed just a little different, everything seemed just a little bit strange.

When Steve got back home to the Hansen family trailer, he seemed to only live for the hour after the family finished supper, around 6:30 or so, when Lisa was most likely to phone him. He spent his days working on the house they were constructing, preferring to work when no one else was around. He found solace in the simple tasks of carpentry, measuring, sawing, hammering and reading the plans for the structure. He could have gone back to work at the mill but, since the whole plan of putting together the adventure company seemed to be down the tubes, he didn't see why he should bother.

In reality, he would much rather be earning some money and spending his weekends with his best friend camping, fishing, hunting and trapping or even practicing some of the more popular activities he wanted to hire himself out to do. But, the way Steve saw his future, it seemed he would be just moving down to Vancouver, hopefully one day soon, and helping Lisa through all her baggage and pain that her injuries, mental and physical, were going to cause her, and perhaps working construction or some such stagnating job somewhere in the city. The incident had caused him to lose about 90% of his hope for the future, and he now rarely even went to visit Smitty and spent more time sneaking drinks and sitting in his room staring at the walls.

When Lisa would call, Steve still wouldn't be that talkative, but he would push himself to sound cheerful and hopeful for her sake. Lisa seemed to be doing better than could be expected and often tried to encourage Steve to think about getting some of the counseling she had. All Steve could think about was the children: the children he would never have.

Yet, for whatever reason, this caused him to be more distant with his younger brother, who didn't seem to totally understand what was going on, except that a lot had changed in a short time, and that he was sad for what his older brother was going through.

Finally, Steve had built up the courage to do what he had wanted to do all along. He was going to see Yuri Molnar. The waiting period had two purposes: one, was so that Steve could have time to think of what he was going to ask and what he was going to say when replied to; and the other, was so that if things got sticky, he wouldn't be bringing down too much heat on himself or the Molnar family from acting too fast for any potential witnesses to connect the events. Steve knew that whatever happened, it would bring some heavy shit down on someone.

It was late one night, near dark, which came at almost 9p.m. at that time of year in that part of the world, when Steve walked up the path of the Molnar house, on the other side of the Town of Walker Lake. He had taken a roundabout way in his dad's truck to get there and walked the last mile or two to their door. He knocked on the door of the older but immaculately kept house and Yuri answered. He smiled when he saw Steve and hoped it was a social visit, as he hadn't had many since they had finished school.

"Stevie!" Yuri said, with a bit of an accent. "Long time no see! Come in, come in! I am just finished my studies. Come join my daddy and me for a drink!" Steve could tell Yuri had already had a drink or two, though out of caution, Steve hadn't had any that night.

"Yeah, buddy," Steve replied, "it has been ages! What are you studying?"

"I am studying a correspondence course from Russia. One day I am going to be big shot in our former home!"

"That's great, dude. I hate to say it though, but I actually came on serious business. Is your dad in right now?"

"Yuri!" Came a yell from what had to be his father. "Who's at the door?" He said, the words spoken in a thick accent.

"Friend of mine, poppa." Yuri replied.

"Bring in your friend: let me meet him!" Molnar said, in a chiding voice.

"Well, it seems he wants to meet you too! Poppa, it is Stevie from my school."

"Actually, I thought I would come talk to the both of you, if it's okay," Steve said.

"Sure, sure. What is on your mind, my friend?" Yuri replied, guiding Steve into the kitchen, where a half-empty bottle of vodka, Yuri's dad and a few glasses, were to be found, not to mention a very nasty-looking revolver. Some of the glasses had vodka in them and some didn't.

"Do you like vodka, Mr. Steve?" Molnar asked.

"Occasionally," Steve lied. He took a glass that Yuri's father offered him with about two ounces of the powerful liquid in it and knocked it straight back.

"I like your friend, Yuri," Molnar said, cracking a wide smile and tipping back a glass of his own in the same fashion. All of a sudden, Molnar picked up the revolver and fired it at something on the floor, making Steve nearly shit himself. "Steve, what brings you to my simple home? Yuri, my boy, please pick up that mouse."

"I have a problem or two." Steve spoke, drawing strength from the vodka. "You see, just a short while ago, I had some dreams: a young girlfriend with a baby on the way, plans for a business that would allow me to do the things I loved around the people I loved. Then, someone came along and took it all away." As he was saying this, he could see a look of disgust come across Molnar's face.

"I don't know if you have to say any more, my friend," Molnar stated. "Yuri!" He said stiffly.

"Yes, father?" Yuri answered.

"Is this the boy whose girlfriend you spoke to me about?" He asked, looking and sounding quite serious.

"I don't know for sure, poppa," Yuri said. "Steve, is Lisa the girlfriend you speak of; the girl we were in school with?"

Steve took the vodka bottle and poured another double, drank it and put down his glass a bit hard, the sound seemingly answering the question posed. He seemed to choke back the pain he felt, and choke slightly on the vodka. "Yes," was all he said.

"I heard about this. I am very sorry for your loss, my friend. What is it that you came here to ask me?"

"I want to pay you to train me so I can set things straight. Lisa was beaten so badly, she can't –we – can't have children. I was thinking maybe you could show me a few things-a few tricks. I can pay you well. I was thinking what I should do is see to it that I return the favor to this piece of scum that did this to her. The police don't want to do anything," Steve replied, looking back and forth at both of the fire-hardened warriors before him with all the seriousness he could muster.

Mr.Molnar was silent for a few moments. He tilted his head, nodded and seemed to be deep in thought for a few more moments. He then cracked a small smile, extended his hand to Steve and said, "This, I can do for you, young man. This I can do. And I will do it for free. My boy Yuri told me about how you were a good friend to him, when many weren't. That counts for a great deal to a man such as me. Also, I lost a wife some years ago. But you have to accept me, just as if you were a soldier and I was your sergeant. You have to follow every order I give you, and if I don't think you are ready to carry out this...operation, you have to accept that. Can you do that?"

"I think I can do just about anything, at this point, Mr. Molnar."

"Be here at 5:30a.m. tomorrow, ready to run. Each day, for a while we will run and, if you don't make it on time one day, or don't follow my orders, I will assume you don't want me to help you anymore. Sleep well, my young friend. A great deal of things are about to change for you, starting tomorrow," Molnar said, with a Cheshire-cat smile, as he lit up a thin cigar and pushed another double over to Steve, who drank it as he had drank the others.

When Steve got home that night, he walked silently past his parents to his room. The last thing he wanted to let on was that he had driven his dad's truck home, drunk on vodka. His inebriated mind came up with all kinds of weird outcomes to his present situation, as he lay down in bed, thinking before he went to sleep. What was this training going to be like? How was he going to get revenge in such a way that, there wouldn't be retaliations to his family and Lisa? He stared up at the ceiling thinking for quite some time before he felt ready to allow himself to sleep. Even when he did eventually drift off, he was greeted with nightmares about how he would feel about doing something that could land him in prison, perhaps even for the rest of his life. These dreams were interspersed with others about Lisa, images of a stillborn child, and the pain he felt about letting them both down as their protector. Despite the horrible dreams, before he knew it, the sun was coming up, he was sober, and it was time to leave for the Molnar residence. He ate what he could, but had a hard time keeping much down, as he was a bit nauseated and hung over. Then, he went out and got his bike, unlocked it and headed off towards his destination, down the long, pine-tree lined hill and through town, and into the Molnar property.

It was about 5:25a.m. when he got to his new teacher's house. He had hoped to have been there earlier, but he purposely made his ride leisurely knowing full well he could be hung out to dry as far as exercise goes. Molnar was waiting in the yard, smoking a thin cigar, smiling and looking at his watch. He knew how much vodka the boy had drank and had his doubts that he would be ready for his training session, but here he was. Molnar had done this on purpose, just to see if Steve was serious, because if he wasn't, he wouldn't last two hours and he would bring trouble down on the senior Molnar, as well.

"Come, my boy, come. Set your bike here by the window and I will show you best way to stretch like proper Russian soldier," said the aging but surprisingly fit gentleman in his characteristic accent. He brought Steve through stretches the young man had done many times in school sports, but much slower and deliberate. Molnar encouraged him to push himself a bit, hurt himself, even. When he was showing Steve stretches, he had no reservations about being aggressive and causing pain. He knew enough not to hurt the boy, but as he had learned, and as he had believed was the best way to learn, a little pain makes a lesson stick. After a good half hour of these stretches, he told Steve, "Now we run. I will lead and I will set pace. This is not a race, but you must keep up. Stay behind and keep your eyes open; we will be going over unfamiliar terrain."

With no further words, the former Soviet Special Forces man threw down his cigar that he had been smoking throughout the stretches, and switched into some kind of hypnotic mode that seemed to tune out everything out, then ran off in the direction of the high ground of the relatively short mountain his property existed on. Steve followed suit, and though the pace of the run started off slower than he was used to running, the difficulty that the increasing altitude caused soon made him grateful he wasn't completely out of shape. They went on and on, upwards and around the back of this mountain, which was around a third the size of the tall peaks in view around Walker Lake. Still, navigating the terrain proved to be incredibly daunting.

On and on they went, over rocks and streams, through thick forest and up, and up, pounding a staccato beat with their steps. It didn't take long for Steve to get his arms and legs cut up from branches and bushes they ran past. A couple of times he even had to push himself hard to catch up after he had twisted an ankle on a rock and slipped, just about falling on his ass. After what seemed like a grand total of two or more hours, they returned to their starting point and, despite his smoking habit, Molnar wasn't even breathing hard at all. Steve was nearly a wreck, having torn his cheap jogging suit in a few places. He felt so exhausted and winded from the run he was bent over, hands on his knees panting and trying to spit all the mucous out of his throat and mouth.

"Good, you did good, my friend," Molnar stated. "No one I have taken on that run made it as far as you did. You should be proud. Now get ready to start training."

"Start? I thought that was training!" Steve exclaimed.

"That, my young friend, was not training. That was your test to see if you could handle training. Tomorrow, when we run, it will be training." The reply came from the Russian as he casually pulled out a fresh cigar.

"Sure, okay. Sounds good. Just give me a couple of seconds," Steve stated, panting away still.

"Mr. Steve, if you are going to do what you want to do, you won't have a couple of seconds. If dogs or men with guns are chasing you, you will not have a couple of seconds. If someone discovers what you are doing and comes up behind you with a baseball bat, there will not be any seconds. You come inside and come now," Molnar stated, seemingly not caring one way or the other, and then walked off towards the house. Steve said nothing and followed him, panting and wheezing.

Inside, down in the basement where Molnar went, there were full length mirrors, several of them on the walls, a weight set, a wrestling mat, and a heavy bag that looked like it had been punched and kicked a few times, already, if the tape and patching was any indicator. The first thing Molnar, did was put Steve through more stretches, slow and deliberate, lasting longer than stretches he had been used to. These stretches mimicked Karate routines he had learned as a child, and he could tell they would make for effective fighting moves as the stretches progressed. This time, the focus was on the upper body, then the former elite soldier put Steve through the rigors of a mid-weight, high repetition, workout. At first Steve, thought the relatively low weight Molnar had put on was a joke, but when he had to bench-press it a hundred times, it didn't seem so funny. Next, he was put through every exercise with weights he had ever done, and more, until his muscles felt like rubber that he no longer had control over. When he was done these, Molnar sent him upstairs to take a bath with Epsom salts to curb the inevitable pain he was going to feel after any period of rest he would take. He was told to take his bath, relax in it for a half hour, then return to the basement. The hot bath felt like heaven. Steve could remember no run, no game of football, or hockey or anything that had taken so much out of him. Still, when he got out and stretched a bit more, he felt he had a little reserve left. Thank goodness he did, Steve thought to himself. He still had to cycle home.

When Steve finally returned to the basement, Molnar had a sort of tangy orange juice drink he gave to Steve without a word, and then, after finishing this, the first thing Steve was told was to take off his shirt and stand in front of the mirror. What his elder trainer said to him then seemed weird, but for whatever reason, he knew this guy had a few things on the ball and was worth listening to.

"Look into the mirror. Do not move; do not think. Breathe in deep through your nose, and out through your mouth. Feel your strength; feel your body. It is a piece of iron. You are a piece of iron. You cannot be destroyed. You are the destroyer. Feel yourself growing stronger: you will not hear words that say there is anything you can't do. You will not hear words that tell you you are wrong, that you can fail. You are a machine made to kill, and to kill quick, and retreat alive. Repeat these words in your head: you are a machine; a solid piece of iron." Molnar said these words, then let Steve say them in his head. After around a half an hour of Steve standing silent, forming the images in his head as he was told, Molnar clapped his hands and dismissed Steve, with strict instructions to return at the same time tomorrow morning.

Steve dressed silently and departed, already feeling that inside of his soul he was somehow changing, changing into something he couldn't quite put a finger on, and that somehow he liked on the surface, but deep down he wondered to himself if he really was a 'killer'.

As Steve rode his bike home, physically he felt like a million bucks. He had used every muscle in his body and he felt as though he could go back for more. Aside from that, he had so much energy his ride went past in no time, and he arrived home in time for supper, then waited for Lisa to call. He spoke to her only for a short time, and was talkative in a positive way as they spoke. He wanted to go to his room and take out his stash of booze and have a drink or two to get himself off to sleep, but as soon as he got near the bed, he felt overpoweringly tired and went right to sleep from 6:00p.m. until 4:00a.m., the next morning. He woke up sore, but stretched in the slow and deliberately timed way he had done the day before, and started off to the other side of town on his bike, feeling better than he had in a long time on the outside, but feeling somehow hollow on the inside. He had such mixed emotions, wondering how many people, in war or otherwise that his trainer had really killed and what that was like. He didn't want to have to kill anyone, but he had some pretty macabre plans in his head to assure no reprisals came his way.

When he arrived at the Molnar residence that morning, much of him was sore and tired, but the stretches helped a lot. It was a good feeling to feel new muscles being formed and being pushed to come out. Steve wondered to himself what lovemaking would be like after a couple of weeks of this level of training. The pristine mountain air and the high protein breakfast of steak and eggs he had ingested gave him a feeling of freedom and energy that he hadn't known before in his young life.

Chapter Seven

The second day of training proved to be quite a bit more difficult for Steve. The workout had its good side though, when it began and the two warriors were running, Steve started to notice some kind of change coming over him, as he pushed himself further and further. The scenery around him, the tall pine trees, the peaks of which he would view as they jogged past, seemed to become more beautiful, more crisp and clean – everything seemed like some kind of spectacular movie playing itself out all around him. He felt so alert and alive, like a wild mustang charging through a valley. Steve began to forget about Sean for a short while and just revel in the feeling, the moment. For that moment, he felt kind of a sense of love for all creation. He had a chance to think about the things that he had done in his life and the times that were to come. When he didn't think about Sean and the revenge he wanted, things seemed to make so much more sense. Unfortunately, the feeling didn't last long.

Steve and Mr.Molnar finished their run. Steve was winded, but a little more prepared for the weightlifting that would come next. When he stopped running, Steve leaned over, hands resting just above his knees, panting a little, sweating a lot. After a few minutes, expecting to be herded into the weight room in the Molnar basement, Steve looked around, and Molnar was nowhere to be seen. All he heard was a footstep behind him, and before he could gather his thoughts enough to turn around, he felt an arm deftly reach around his neck, and put him into a chokehold. Then, with more seeming ease, the arm lifted his whole body off the ground and it felt like his neck was going to break. All he could do was gurgle. Then, just as suddenly as it grasped him, Steve was let go by the brawny arm and fell to the ground, coughing and spitting.

"Shit! What was that for?" Steve exclaimed.

"That is lesson number one: how to break your enemy's neck. You like?" Molnar said, grinning, seeming quite pleased with himself. "Remember, my young friend: this person who hurt your woman, killed your child – he does not play by the rules, and so, I can only harm you if I don't show you every trick I know. Now get up and put me into the same headlock."

"With pleasure, sir!" Steve said, scrambling to his feet. He circled around, crouched down while Molnar stood confidently looking off in another direction. Steve knew the old man was in shape, so he grabbed him roughly with his strong right arm and tried to lift.

In response, the former Spetznatz soldier stepped backwards with his left foot, changing his centre of gravity to make the lifting headlock impossible, then lifted his right foot and brought it down hard on Steve's right instep. As Steve cringed in pain, Molnar curled and crouched with him, gaining enough advantage to reach back, grab his assailant's head and arm, and flip him right over himself, causing the boy to land on his back.

"Lesson number two is how to get out of such a headlock. I am sorry, my friend, but I have to teach you what warfare is like. If I fail to do so, and you are injured or die, I will feel very bad. Now take a break, get some water from my kitchen, and wait for me there." Steve got to his feet grudgingly and headed towards the house. Molnar lit up another thin cigar and stood, feeling quite happy looking out at the tall peaks and the seemingly endless numbers of pine trees taking root as high up on the sides of the mountains as mother nature would allow. In some ways, Molnar saw himself as similar to these pine trees. There were many people out there who had wished him silenced years ago, when his country no longer needed him. There were even more who actually thought he was dead. This new inspiration he was feeling to train this determined young man, gave him a lot of ideas. Like the pine trees on the peaks, maybe there was a place for an aging, unwanted old war-horse like himself. He thought back to his army days and wondered what had brought him here to this place, the rocky mountains, so harsh and so beautiful. Maybe it was fear. Maybe it was suggested to him that he go here, because the only real authority in such a place was the wilderness: the final judge and arbiter of a man's soul. A part of him missed his more active days and the battles he had fought; the friends he had lost. Time was a cruel taskmaster. Maybe this would be his last borderline legal undertaking. Such jobs as this had made him rich, but even his tortured Russian soul wanted forgiveness, redemption. If only he knew where to find these things.

When Steve got to the kitchen, he took some cold, clear water from the fridge jug and felt its replenishing power run through him as he satiated his deep thirst. He sat down at the table upon which sat a chess board, all set up and ready to be played. He studied it, thinking of the rules he didn't completely remember, and the games he used to play against the computers at school when his computer teacher wasn't looking. Soon Molnar came in, and asked, in his thick accent, "You play chess my, young friend?"

"Just a little. And not for a long time," Steve replied.

"Then you will learn; is best game for a warrior's mind. Strike without losing. Dominate. Win. It is all here, 32 black and 32 white places: the whole world. Russian children learn this game before leaving diapers. Come, you play first." Molnar turned the wooden board so that the white pieces were on Steve's side of the table. Steve put his hand to his chin and stared for a few awkward minutes at the playing surface. He opened by moving out his queen's knight.

"Is good move sometimes, for beginners. Sadly, I am not beginner." Molnar moved out a pawn one space forward, not the two he could have moved it. The pawn was directly in front of his black king. Steve noted that his king was now exposed to attack and moved the pawn in front of his king's knight two spaces, in hopes of later moving out his bishop to attack the exposed black monarch. Then Molnar brought out his king's bishop to the middle of the table.

Something clicked when Molnar did this. Steve had seen this combination before: it was known as the three-move checkmate. Next, the old man would bring out his queen, then strike at the pawn beside the king's pawn, and the game would be over. The king wouldn't be able to take the piece that threatened him because it was guarded by the other piece, and neither would any of the pieces around the king, being locked in their starting positions. The defense was simple: bring out the queen's pawn one space and the move wouldn't work. Steve moved the piece and Molnar laughed out loud.

"Yes, my young friend. You have played before. Well done, well done." The game continued and it didn't take many more moves for Steve to be checkmated. When it was over, Molnar said to Steve, "You will learn more as we go, Steve. You can feel proud: you showed me you can think. Now, next time I sneak up behind you, try to get my foot like I did yours, and always be ready for an attack. How does your foot feel now?"

"It's better. A bit numb, but better," Steve replied.

"You can soak again, later. Now, have some vodka and then, we will lift more weights." Molnar stood, took a bottle from the cupboard and two glasses, and poured a shot for each of them. They both downed their shots, then stood and headed down for the basement. The workout, though more difficult this time, seemed to go past quickly. Again, Molnar had Steve soak in his tub, then stand in front of a mirror silently as he power-talked him into some confidence and self-esteem in what Molnar had known as 'the warrior way'.

Steve looked into the mirror and seemed to gain knowledge about his physical body as he looked at it. He could see his growing muscles, his scratches and bruises, he spent some time simply being aware of his breathing, and he mentally rehearsed the moves he had been shown earlier. All these things went through his head, but what he mostly thought about was facing down Sean. What would he do? How would he do it? In this respect, Steve was a bit lost, but he knew he was doing the right thing. If he was doing nothing else, he was unloading a lot of the energy he would have spent obsessing on what he would do to Sean and the repercussions of what Sean had done to him and Lisa. Soon the day's training was over, and he was riding his bike back to Green Mountain Road; this time, focusing more on setting a pace, being aware of his surroundings, and meditating in his own way on what he was learning and why he was learning it.

When Steve got home, he lost himself again in a few hours of work on the house. His dad was starting to wonder when he would go back to work at the sawmill, if ever, and his mom asked him a few questions about where he was going during the day. Steve tried to not say anything, but he let it slip that he had been working out and trying to sort stuff out. That was more than he wanted to say; his mom had a habit of giving away information to people around town whenever they asked, and he didn't want to do anything to reveal Molnar's identity as his trainer. After supper, Lisa called and she seemed to be a bit sad. Steve asked her what questions he could. He tried to encourage her in what she was trying to do but didn't let on that he hated the idea of living in Vancouver. After a few 'I love you' and 'I miss you' phrases, he hung up, feeling a bit overcome by his day, so he went right to his room, had a few sips of vodka and fell into a deep sleep once again.

Chapter Eight

As more days and more rigorous training sessions went past, things pretty much went as they did for the first two days. Always the run in the morning, seemingly so soon after his ride to the Molnar's place. And in the evening, his heart-felt talks with Lisa that Steve often nearly missed. After the run though, there was chess, mental conditioning, and then weights, and more mental conditioning. Every now and then, Molnar would throw Steve a curve ball and take a swing at him, or throw him over his shoulder, or even run faster and faster, leaving Steve far behind. Soon, Steve grew used to the training, and even started to anticipate when his trainer was going to hit him, or sneak in another move. There was always more to learn, everything from defending from and initiating knife attacks, to lessons on rifles and pistols of all types and sizes. How to use them, aim them, clean them, and how to un-jam them in seconds. Though Molnar had many guns, they were only really able to shoot pellet guns for target practice, since buying large amounts of ammunition and firing off same would attract too much attention. The effect was achieved though, and Molnar could see in Steve's eyes that mentally and physically he was turning into the professional killer he had once sought to turn himself into. For a while, the younger of the two had no idea when the training would end; it was kind of left up in the air. But the day Steve beat Molnar at chess, four games out of five, the former soldier knew it was time to start making plans on how Steve was going to get his final revenge.

Molnar told Steve that the best time for them to strike was at night, and that it was exceedingly important for them to learn Sean's movements and activities. So the first evening after Steve was told he was nearly ready, they went to stake out the house in which Steve's mortal enemy lived. Each and every move, from when Sean's parents turned off their TV and put the dog out, to how long they took to prepare for bed and turn off the lights, was documented as the two lay in sleeping bags, Steve with binoculars and Molnar with a night vision scope.

Steve was really beginning to feel, after all he had been through, that he could just walk up and beat the crap out of this guy. But Molnar would have none of it. They would wait diligently and then work out a plan. He had lost too many friends from boldness in the years the Russian army had tried to control Afghanistan, and other places Molnar had once wanted to forget, but now kind of missed. He told this Steve, when the young man started to seem edgy and impulsive about what they were doing. Molnar had seen a lot of himself in Steve; he would have willingly gone into combat with him, he thought to himself, which was perhaps the highest indication of respect an old soldier like him could bestow upon a person.

After they returned from their ongoing reconnaissance mission, the two would catch a couple of hours sleep, then go for their run together. The two of them were beginning to turn into a cohesive team, which was perhaps why Molnar decided he was going to go along with Steve when he finally made his move. It was a lot more likely though that he had decided to go along because, after all his adventures in battle, and being trained by what he felt was the finest force of soldiers in the world, the idea of going into action again was appealing enough to risk what he had built for himself and his son here in Canada.

The plan was simple. They would go to Sean's house at night, going into action after everyone had gone to sleep. They would disperse a type of gaseous formula Molnar had made out of a few household and non-household chemicals on both of Sean's parents, and most likely Sean himself, by expelling with a portable large sized pump operated atomizer. Then, they would tie up Sean while he was unconscious, and put him in the trunk of a car they would rent or buy cheap at some place, far enough away to not easily implicate them, if things went wrong. Fake identification would be needed, which was solved when an Alberta Driver's License and Alberta Health care card arrived in the mail from an old family friend of the Molnar's. This was the final step before taking action on their plan. They would then take him to a deserted barn Molnar knew of, and then, from that point, it was up to Steve what would be done with him. Nothing really scared the old Russian anymore, after what he had done and seen in the name of the Union of Soviet Socialist Republics; but, he hoped the punishment would fit the crime, as the senior Molnar family member was honestly starting to care about the boy, and grow more disgusted at the young man who had driven him to an extreme of hate-filled lust for revenge.

In order to prepare themselves for the task at hand, the two of them practiced on the Molnar residence. They got Yuri to change the furniture around each time and they would wait out in the nearby forest after dark and practice opening the window and creeping around undetected in low light, with gas masks and filtered flashlights. Soon, their timings and performance got good enough, that they were confident they could pull off their own little version of small town justice.

Although they hadn't spoken much in the past while, Steve was able to convince his friend Smitty to ride the bus as far out of town as he could, pick up a newspaper, and find in it a $500.00 car they could use for their attack, which they would later pick up and insure and register with their new identification cards. They had decided renting a car would leave too much of a paper trail and attract attention they didn't want or need. A cheap car could be disposed of at the bottom of a lake. A rental car would be wanted back and would be looked for even if it was simply late. It was a wise decision because most rental cars had GPS trackers in them that would detail everything they were to do with it. The owner of the car they eventually picked tried to put it across as a combination Ferrari-BMW when in fact it was just a thirty year-old Datsun. He was visibly surprised when Steve bought it after kicking a side panel and having a rusty piece of metal fall from inside the panel on the ground. They spent the next few days fixing the car to be reliable enough for the job and painting and even denting it, so it didn't resemble itself from even a few days before.

With this done, Steve and Molnar decided that the best night to move would be Sunday, and the best time to move would be at about 4 a.m.. This timing made it more possible their victim would be home sleeping off a bender and there would perhaps also be less attention paid to anyone driving around at that hour. Molnar told Steve to go home and get as much rest as he could over the next few days and so, he headed off home feeling strong, feeling confident, and feeling ready. When Lisa called up that night, he tried to tell her what was going to happen without really telling her what was happening.

"Lisa! How are things going?"

"Good. Really good. I think I'm close to being ready."

"Ready? How so?"

"I think I'm ready for you to come down here and stay with me, Stevie."

"That's awesome. What brought this on?"

"Well, I wasn't sure until just a short while ago then, I started thinking about you and Colin and your mom and dad, and how much you do for all of us, and how much you care. I prayed for awhile, just like my counselor told me to, and I just sort of felt ready."

"I've been thinking too, sweetie. I've been thinking that, maybe after staying down there for a while, we could come back and live in the trailer here; give Walker Lake another chance. You're right about me caring for my family, and all. I love them a lot and I don't want to lose them, or do without them. Also, I have been thinking a lot about that adventure company we talked about. We can't do that in Vancouver."

"No, Stevie, you can't do it here, but you can start up a small store selling adventure goods and become an outfitter. You could even start tours going out of town for bungee jumping, and camping and hiking and stuff. I met this friend here, and she told me there are tons of places for that around Vancouver, and the competition for guides is fairly low."

"Really?" Steve thought for a minute. For that brief amount of time, he wondered what would happen if he didn't seek revenge – if he tried what Lisa said. It could make his whole life easier: it would take the knot that had formed in his stomach since the day his 'official' training had completed, and he wouldn't have to worry what would happen if he were caught or if something went wrong. Unfortunately, the thought only lasted for that one minute. "Lisa, I will think about it, okay? But, I'm working on something right now; I'm working on something that would make it safe for you to come back. This guy is a coward, beating on a young woman like you. All he needs is some sense taught to him and things will be all right."

"Steve? You don't mean you are still going to...you said you wouldn't do anything, Stevie! What if you get caught...what if this guy strikes back at you? What if he tries something on your family – or mine? Did you think of that?"

"I thought of it, Lisa. I thought a lot about it and I don't think I'm going to give him any chance to pull something like that. This is something I have to do. For you. For us."

"For us? I thought you were better than that macho bullshit, Stevie – that's what I used to like about you. Don't you know what 'turn the other cheek' means? If not for yourself, for me! Think about it before you're in too deep!"

"I made up my mind, Lisa and I'm not going to just let this go unpunished. You tell me this is about you; what about our baby – my baby? Don't you know what it means if we let this go? He'll end up doing it to someone else. You will end up living in Vancouver and not only will I hate every bit of it and want to just come home, I will curse myself forever for letting that asshole get away with hurting you and killing our child! I can't let that happen, trouble or no trouble."

"What are you going to do?" Lisa asked, choking back her tears.

"I'm going to put the fear of God into him. And if I hear of him pulling any more of these stunts, I'm going to make sure he never has another chance to even try one."

"Are you insane? If you do this, you'll lose me."

"I've already lost you, Lisa." Steve could hardly believe how cold and hardened he had become, even to someone he cared so deeply about. With those words, Steve hung up the cordless phone and walked into the kitchen, where Frank, Ruth and Colin were.

His Mother asked, "Are you going to your friend's place to stay again?"

"In a couple of days probably," Steve said, somewhat sheepishly.

"Good, you're going to be around. Your father wants some help with the new house tomorrow, then, the day after that, we were going to drive you to Vancouver, so you can see Lisa. How would you like that?"

"I don't think I'll be seeing Lisa anymore, Mom. We just had a talk." His three family members looked up at him, with a bit of a look of shock on their faces. After a few seconds of not knowing what to say or do, his mother stood up and went to him to talk to him in private and try and find out what was happening. A lot of strange stuff had been going on, from the vodka bottles they had found or noticed in the recycling, to the long periods he would spend with his new friend whom he refused to talk about. They were starting to get a little more than concerned.

"It's okay. It's been coming for a while. I was ready for this," Steve said, still with a blank look on his face. "I just can't see myself leaving Walker Lake, right now. Maybe she'll come around and discover how much it means to me-maybe she won't. Either way, I have to take care of a few things around town."

"Whatever you want, Stevie, we'll stay behind you," his mom said, hugging him as she did. "We'll do anything to help you, just be honest with us as much as you can. And think about the things you are doing. No good comes out of plans made when you are emotional."

Steve looked down, knowing he had to be far from honest to them about a lot of things, then smiled and hugged his mom back. "I will Mom. You know I love you and Dad and Colin too much to hurt you or lie to you." Even that was kind of a lie, Steve thought to himself. He said no more and went into his room and laid down for a long time. He thought about the last time he had been with Lisa, and wondered to himself why he had to give that up – just so he could prove to some asshole that he couldn't be fucked with. He also thought for a long time about what he saw when he looked into Molnar's eyes: that sick bloodlust, that deadness. What was he doing? This would never end until someone got killed, or until he himself went to jail. All of a sudden, he thought about how much of a crush he used to have on Lisa and how she accepted him as a forgiving person, a good person. He picked up the phone and dialed Lisa.

"Hello?" Lisa answered her phone.

"Hi, Lisa. It's Steve."

"Stevie! I was hoping you would call back. You have to be honest with me. You have to call off your plans right now!"

"I know, I know. I just...things are..."
"What have you gotten yourself into?"

"I had a friend from school. His dad was training me so I could get this guy, do something to him."

"Something...what kind of something?

"We were going to kidnap him and cut off his testicles."

"Are you insane? How do you think you could cover that up? I know he's a bastard, but for Heaven's sake he's a human being! He could die and then you would go down for murder. They don't stop looking for murderers, you know, and you would be the prime suspect."

"I know, I know. I just..."
"You just what?"

"I just don't care, I wanted so much to live with you, love you, raise kids. Here. Now, that it isn't possible. All I've been able to think about was Sean."

"Steve, if you ever want me back, if you ever want a chance at something, you have to call the police. You have to turn yourself in."

"I know, I know, Lisa...but this Molnar guy, he's a true killer. He...I know." Steve began to weep. He felt friendless, totally alone in the world, thinking about what he had to do. Then he thought about all the times he had with Lisa, all the lovemaking and long talks and camping trips, the days they were friends. He decided he would do it. He would stop this before it got anywhere. "Okay, Lisa, for you. I'll call the cops, tell them everything. I have to go. I need to drive over to the RCMP station. I might get some time though – I was a part of this."

"Stevie, I know you can get through it. But don't just call the police. Go and talk to your parents about this; get them on your side. And don't forget that I'll be here. Call me as soon as you can. No matter what happens, I'll be with you, Steve, forever.

Steve just hung up the phone, went into where his parents were sitting, and borrowed the keys to his dad's truck. He then decided he might not be coming back, so he asked his mom and dad to come with him. Before even starting the engine, he leaned his head on the steering wheel, and tried to hold back the pain and tears.

"Dad, Mom...did you ever have something that hurt so much you nearly let it destroy you?" Steve said first in the still thick silence of the night.

"I did once, many years ago, before I came here, to Walker Lake," His dad said, knowing a powder keg was about to go off in his truck.

"Can you talk about it?'

"Steve, what in hell is going on with you? You have been so messed up I don't know whether to put you into some kind of counseling or bend you over my knee and whip you."

"You might as well know; everyone is going to know. I got this former army guy to train me, and he was going to help me get revenge on the guy that beat up Lisa. I want to put a stop to it, but it may have gone to far, so I'm going to the cops."

"I just about figured that much. You should have come to us sooner, Son. I don't know how I can help you anymore."

"Just be my Dad. That's all I can ask."

Chapter Nine

After a lot of talking and a long, slow drive to the RCMP detachment, Steve pulled into the parking lot of the building, a one story structure in the middle of downtown, and walked out of the truck, wishing he had thought to have a drink or had brought some vodka. This he was going to have to face sober, though. He went inside and there was the same officer that had spoken to him and Smitty in the hospital, months back.

"Hi there. Steve, isn't it?" Sergeant Johnson said, as he stood up from his desk and extended a hand to Steve and his dad, while his mom stayed in the background. "What can I help you with?"

"Two things, sir: one, I need to report a crime, and two, I want to turn myself in for my part in it."

"Why do I have a sneaking feeling this has to do with the first time you and I met?" the officer replied.

"It does, sir. I had made plans to get my revenge since you and I had first met. Serious revenge, and I found someone who wants to take it a lot further. Things seem to have gotten so out of hand, that I don't know what to do anymore, and I am hoping you can stop him before someone gets hurt or worse."

"I hate to tell you this, Steve, but we just about know all about it."

Steve's eyes widened and his blood ran cold, as if he wasn't nervous enough. "Can you give me an idea of what you know, so I can try and help stop this?"

"That's a generous offer. Well, we know you have been associating with the Molnar family. I personally took an interest in this case and looked him up. He has a legal driver's license and passport in the name of Molnar, and his property is registered to Mr. Molnar, but other than that, Mr. Molnar doesn't exist."

"In what way?"

"In the way that he can be tracked by police computers. So I did a little footwork and when he went to the liquor store I watched him as he handled a couple of bottles, then bought them so I could get prints off of them. It isn't exactly good enough for court purposes, but then when I found out some of the things this guy has done I didn't think he was in any position to bring a privacy case against me. I ran the prints through our computer, and, again, nothing."

"Okay, so how often does this sort of thing happen?"

"With former Soviets? Never. They are fingerprinted right when they try to immigrate. So, I called up the boys from CSIS in Ottawa, sent them what I had, and they had some interesting things to say about your friend."

"I do too, and I don't have a lot of time."

"Mr. Molnar, as you know him, doesn't exist. Mr. Kevlov is an actual former Soviet who immigrated some time ago and disappeared. But not before being a suspect in two murder cases. He's been quiet for some time, but the men at CSIS are very interested in the fact that he has come out of retirement. We wanted to intervene sooner, but we have a lot of people to take care of, and few officers. CSIS is keeping an eye on our friend, but, presently, they can't touch him. Their plan was to wait until he killed again and let him think he got away with it, then swoop in. Personally, I think as soon as he was done with your victim, you and him would be on a slow boat to Russia with his son, and the chances that you would ever come back would be close to nil."

"Do cops actually make people wear a wire?"

"Hidden microphone? Yes, at times."

"What would happen if I wore one, and got him to admit to his crimes, before he can do anything to that rapist bastard. What if I can get him for you?"

"Well, that would be a very valuable piece of information."

"Valuable enough for me to escape prosecution?"

"I personally couldn't guarantee it, but if you get him before he does anything technically, you wouldn't have done anything wrong. I would have no cause to even arrest you. You would have to testify, though," the officer replied

"Does the RCMP have any kind of witness protection program?"

"I'm not really the person to talk to about it. It certainly isn't like the things you see on TV, but I can answer some general questions."

"Well, with what I'm going to have to risk is there a way I can get a place to live in Vancouver and about $20,000.00?"

"It's definitely possible. I've heard of cases like that, but remember that if you fail and you don't get us our man or you try to screw us, you would get nothing. But if you do get us Kevlov, I can see what can be done."

"And what if my son ends up getting killed or crippled trying this insane stunt?" Steve's dad interjected.

"That is a risk only you and your son can decide on taking, but I have to remind you, that if Kevlov gives us the slip, or is alerted to our knowledge of his present situation, our friends in CSIS could very literally be out for someone to prosecute. The way they will see it is that if they can get to Steve and use it as leverage on other pending cases, they will gladly throw the book at him in court."

"Steve," asked his father, "come outside with your mother and I. Let's talk about this for just a few minutes."

"Sure, that sounds like a good idea."

The three got outside and Steve noticed right away that his mom was crying and his dad's eyes were beginning to moisten as well.

"Stevie," his dad said, "I want you to know that I love you. Maybe more than I love anyone except, maybe your mother and Colin who stand equal. I want to say that I am very proud of you, but you don't have to go all the way with this. This Russian is a crazy psychopath, from what I understand, and if you face off to him, there are all kinds of reasons he might want to kill you, and I don't want that to happen. If things have gone this far, maybe you should just let the chips fall where they may, go into custody now, give evidence and let the police handle this monster. I can't face losing you, Stevie."

"I can't face it either, Son," his mom said, "But if this is what you want to do, you have to do it."

"I love you both so much, but like Dad said about Mom, I think I love Lisa more. I have one chance, one hope that her and I can get together again, and have the life we deserve together. So I'm sorry to both of you, but I have to go through with this. I have to stop this guy and stop him from killing me, or anyone else for that matter. Once this is done, we will all be safe, and if it isn't done, none of us will be. Do you understand?"

"I do, Stevie. just be careful," his Mom said, as she hugged her oldest boy and then let him walk back inside the police station. The two parents stood outside and talked about how Steve was such a wonderful boy growing up, and how they had both known he would make something of himself. A few minutes later, their boy came out and got into the truck, letting his Dad drive and sat in silence, mentally preparing himself for the task he must do.

Steve woke up the next morning at 4:30a.m., to the sound of the phone ringing. He grabbed it before anyone else was awoken by it; it turned out to be Mr. Molnar – or Mr. Kevlov – he thought to himself. He wanted Steve to come by, right away, and so he got on his bike and pedaled away the miles in a half state of anxiety, wondering if the Russian knew what he had agreed to the day before.

It was nice to ride in the cool air, and see the beginning of the outline of the mountains coming, as the sun rose way below their commanding presence. He made it to the house in a relatively short time, and there he was, the man he was about to set up, standing in his workout gear, smoking his little cigar.

"Stevie, my boy, I thought I would catch you off guard and get in a little run and go over our plans. Put your bike anywhere. We will go now."

Steve stashed his bike and did the best he could to follow the Russian murder suspect. The old man put on a good race, speeding through the woods, up the small mountain at much more than his normal pace. They got about two miles into the run, and, all of a sudden, Steve lost sight of his trainer. He kept running, but was much less sure of where he was and where he was going. All of a sudden, he tripped on an unseen stump or tree root – he wasn't sure what it was, but it knocked him to the ground. In a split second, an arm was around him and his head was being smashed into the ground. He gave up resisting and, in the dim light, he could see Kevlov, his large and muscled frame keeping Steve from moving, and the glint of a knife in the dim light.

"Stevie, I have something to discuss with you," the shadow said.

"Y...yes, is the knife really necessary?" Steve replied.

"You tell me boy. Tell me why a friend of mine from town called and mentioned you paid a visit to the police yesterday. Tell me this is nothing, that your good friend Mr. Molnar is not going to have to deal with you."

"I just went to get a hunting license. I didn't say anything."

"I happen to know, Stevie that hunting licenses were being issued weeks ago. Can you tell me why you didn't go get yours then?"

"Yeah, of course. I wanted to make sure the cop didn't know me and didn't ask any funny questions about you or I." Steve lied. "I talked to him. He didn't say anything."

"Yes, this is very smart, my boy, but if you are to do such a thing again, please let me know. We are doing something very dangerous here, and I am helping you. This is my neck that is being risked, too." He put away the knife.

"Can we go back now?" Steve asked. "I could use a little more sleep. I can't see how running more today could help us any."

"Yes, yes, go home and rest. Tomorrow evening it will all come together as we planned. Just one thing: I need to test things out at the barn, just to make sure, will you come here in the morning?"

"I can do that. What time?" Steve replied.
"Ten would be fine; sleep as much as you like."

Steve made his way home, feeling nervous, hungry, and shaky. In the middle of town, he stopped and used a pay phone to call the police. He had no way of knowing if he was being watched or followed, so he talked to the Sergeant Johnson, and asked him to come by with the listening device in plain clothes and not in a police car. The officer agreed, and then Steve went home. He talked to his dad for a while, who really had wanted him to just let the police handle things, but Steve felt he was the only person who the Russian trusted enough to get led into a trap, plus that the cops had said they needed him both as a witness and a person with a listening device. His dad was visibly upset. He hated the idea of one of his loved ones risking their lives, even a little. It had been hard to watch Steve grow up, and become interested in hunting and rock climbing and all the stuff he considered fun, but not useful skills that would get him ahead in life. He, too, despite the hardness of his heart, had said more than a few prayers for Steve in the past while.

All that day, Steve sat in his room, thinking about all that had gone on. Finally he got out a piece of paper and started to write a letter to Lisa, as follows:

Dear Lisa,

I spent a lot of time thinking about what you said to me last time we spoke. With a little help, I made a decision that I wasn't going to carry out my plan. Every bit of me now wants to follow you to Vancouver, start my life fresh, and get over the pain of losing our baby without having to take revenge. I just wish you knew how much I love you, and how important it was to me to get revenge. I went to get help to get back at Sean, but now it seems I am over my head. I am doing something that might get us enough to start anew and start that tour guide business in Vancouver that we talked about, right now. I wouldn't want to do anything more than that. I still dream of the day we say goodnight and don't have to go back to separate homes. I have just one more thing to do here, but I don't know if you will take me back, so I may just stay in town for a while. If anything happens to me, I am making arrangements for you to get a little money that I hope you use to find a better guy than me.

Signed, Steve.

He folded up the letter, placed it in an envelope, put a stamp on it, and rode his bike to town to mail it. When he got back, the RCMP officer from town was there, wearing a baseball cap instead of one of the peaked caps the RCMP normally wore. Like this, the officer looked like an ordinary guy. He showed Steve how to tape on the listening device and showed him a switch that would make it easier for the cops to know where they were located, then wished Steve the best and cautiously drove away.

Steve went into his room and he wrote out who should get his property, which wasn't much. He was feeling scared but also a bit energized about all the things that were going to happen in just one day. Most of his stuff, he left to his younger brother, and the money was to go to Lisa. Steve had his Dad sign the document as a witness and left it in the drawer of his bedside table. Then he took the last couple of drinks from a mickey of vodka he had sitting hidden in his dresser and slipped into a fitful and restless sleep. He had a lot of things to do before he could have this kind of relaxation again.

Steve woke up at around 6:30 a.m. He had wanted to wake up sooner, but his body didn't agree that he had enough sleep. He carefully put on the listening device and then went and got on his bike and rode downtown to call the police station to get confirmation that it was working. They gave quick instructions and a pep talk that he was to in no way endanger himself any more than necessary and gave him the go-ahead. Steve went to the all-night diner on the edge of town and let some greasy eggs slip down his throat and washed it down with some orange juice. He then ordered the same again, when he realized he would be at the Molnar place too early.

"Don't see you around here much," the waitress said as she offered him coffee.

"I live up on the mountain. Mostly eat at home."

"Hey-I think I know you. Steve, right? You were seeing Lisa for the longest time."

"Yeah, that's me. Who might you be?"

"I'm Wanda. Lisa and I used to be friends. Back when she was dating that Sean asshole."

"Hmmm...what's he up to? Haven't heard much about him," Steve probed.

"Oh...didn't you hear? Just a couple of weeks ago he beat up and raped another woman in Oak County. I guess the girl was from the reserve and after he got the shit kicked out of him he got charged. Heard he's going away for good now. Some kids saw the whole thing and his rich Daddy isn't even going to help him with a lawyer. Serves him right, too."

Steve let out a small laugh, then thought about all the pain he was going to cause his family and the pain and trouble he was ready to put himself through, just to prove he was some big man. He thanked the waitress, tipped her well, and got back on his bike.

As he made his way across town, in the cool morning mountain air Steve thought a lot about the things he did in the past while, how he had been trained to be some kind of killer, and all that. He could have a good career in the army, he thought, but he wasn't totally sure he had any room to make plans in his life, considering what he was going to do to the most dangerous man he had ever known. It felt so good to be in shape, so good to run and train, if only he had picked a better way to go about it, a better way to motivate himself. Well, at least he was going to get some money if this all went well.

At around 9:45, Steve arrived at Kevlov's property and no one was in sight. The car they had fixed up was the only thing that didn't make the whole place seem like some kind of ghost town, even the kitchen door was ajar and no lights or sounds were there. He walked up to the door. As he went through, someone or something pulled a sack over his head and started to punch him, repeatedly. He tried yelling and screaming, but nothing seemed to stop his attacker. Then, he was tied up and tossed into the trunk of the car, like he was some kind of rag doll. The car sped off and Steve realized that his secret was out. How Kevlov had found out he didn't know, but what he did know, was that what happened in the next short while would determine whether he lived or died.

As Steve lay in the trunk of the small car, he spoke out each turn to himself, trying to figure out the route the vehicle was taking, and relay it to the police that were hopefully following him. He had no idea that his plan was working, or if the RCMP could even hear him. He spoke out the description of the vehicle; anything that might help find the car he was in. Steve soon began to feel as though he had messed with someone quite a bit smarter than him. He had been taught a lot, but if this man already had two murders or more under his belt, and hadn't been caught, who knows what he was capable of?

After a good hour and a half, the car seemed to turn down a bumpy road and stop shortly after. The trunk opened up and above him, though he couldn't see him, was the former Spetznatz special warfare specialist.

"Stevie, Stevie, Stevie, my boy. You came to me with a problem. I helped you for free, and then you turn on me. I know who is out there: it is someone I only know as Control; he has been looking for me for a long time. I have friends watching him, and then these friends tell me, he has information about me and will likely pay me a visit. Such a strange man, thinking he can stop me. I am going to take care of this man once and for all, and you, my boy, are going to be my bait. You are going to bring him to me." With that, Kevlov picked up Steve and carried him into a large building. He could smell hay and hear birds flying around. This had to be the 'barn' Kevlov had talked about.

The Russian tied Steve firmly to a chair, leaving the sack on his upper body, and then put a rope around the chair and him and threw it over a beam, under the ceiling and pulled it, so Steve and the chair were suspended in the air. Then, all went silent, but the birds. Steve tried to talk to the listening device, hoping that it was still on him.

"Oh my boy, you are a smart one," came Kevlov's voice from another part of the barn. "A listening device. Good trick, I like. But don't say anymore. In case you aren't sure, here." Kevlov got a ladder and climbed up to Steve's height, then a sudden a BANG!! went off right near Steve's ear, making him scream in pain from the extremely loud blast. Next, Kevlov cut open the sack and pulled off the device Steve wore under his shirt. "Ahhh, yes! And a tracking device. This is good. This is very good. I will not have to wait so long for Control to come." Kevlov took more rope and firmly tied up Steve's mouth and threw the device on the dirt floor. Steve could feel blood running out of his ear as once again, his now mortal enemy disappeared and waited, unaffected at the idea that he was going to kill at least one or two people later in the day.

It seemed like a lifetime, but in about twenty minutes or so, Steve first saw vehicles come to a stop outside the barn. A few minutes later, one of the RCMP officers from Walker Lake came and kicked open the door, his pistol at the ready. He saw Steve, all tied up but didn't see anyone else, so he gave a signal to his partner to check around the back of the barn, outside the building. He left and in came another man, tall, wearing a suit that looked like it cost more than the trailer his family lived in. The officer, who turned out to be Sergeant Johnson untied Steve and let him down from the roof but Steve could barely hear his own voice after the pistol had been fired in his ear. He tried sign language at first, but then, drew out on the ground that Kevlov was trying to draw in Control to kill him. Before he could finish though, Steve smelled smoke and looked up, as a torrent of flame engulfed the wall behind them, and the door where they had come in, was slammed shut and on fire itself. Now they were in deep and it seemed as though there was no way out.

Chapter Ten

Without pausing to explain, Steve went back and grabbed the rope he had been suspended from, just minutes before, and carried it up to the barn loft. He swung across the barn on it twice, the second time managing to smash through a window, and then doing his best to land in a soft spot, he let go of the rope outside of the burning barn and ended up on the safer side of the fire. He got into the car he had come there in the trunk of, and drove it through the burning wall, and let in the cop and his friend, and drove back out. He was able to speak just enough after that, to say that he was going after Kevlov, that he was perhaps the only one who could run him down, not to mention that he knew the ground the man would be covering.

Control took a long look at Steve, saw the dedicated look in his eyes, and the personal strength it took to cross a man like Kevlov, then looked at the cop, and nodded. Control reached in his pocket and took out his gun, and handed it to the young man.

Steve took off right away, but as he got around to the back of the barn, there was the second officer, on the ground, bleeding from the belly. The wound wouldn't kill him, but it would slow down anyone who found him, who would stop to care for the wound. Steve just rushed around to the other side of the barn, grabbed the other RCMP officer, and dragged him to the wounded man. Then he took off, hell for leather, towards where he knew Kevlov would be heading.

As Steve ran, the odd bent twig and footprint in the mud gave him a pretty clear path to follow and, a pretty good idea that his instincts were right. If Kevlov had an extra half an hour, he would be able to climb down to lower ground, and bushes and marshes that would hide him and feed him long enough to get away. He didn't have that time, though, and Steve was hot on his trail, pistol in hand.

After a few more minutes of hard running, the trail seemed to end. Could he be hiding? Did he double back? Before he could answer, he figured out what was going on, but it was too late.

Kevlov came crashing down on him, from a high branch of a tree, just above. The two wrestled, first for the gun, then after Steve tossed the gun away, they wrestled for their lives. It was an incredible struggle. Kevlov had the strength of a Russian bear. But Steve was thin and wiry, and nearly as strong. He had never had to fight for his life before, and while they were on the ground, Kevlov put him into a chokehold, as they both lay on their backs, Steve on top of the Russian. Steve used all of his midsection strength and curled up, then flipped back, smashing the back of his head into his enemy's nose, smashing the back of his enemy's head into the ground. Kevlov's grip weakened for just a moment, and Steve rolled away from him, and, in one motion, rose to his feet, and, grabbing the pistol he had thrown, he took the upper hand.

"Alright, Kevlov or Molnar. I'm going to do to you what you least want to happen. I'm going to give you to Control and make you see so much disgrace, you'll spend the next 20 years in prison, wishing you had never been born."

"Stevie. Stevie," Kevlov answered in his thick accent. "You know this will not happen. I'll bet you thought I was coming here to get away. I am now going to tell you that with Control, you never get away. He is an agent – CIA – and he has ways to turn my brain to goop to try and get useless secrets out of me. He is a man who should have died in the Cold War; he would have been happier that way. Me, I just try to help my friends. You were my friend, Stevie."

"Just shut the fuck up and stay right there," Steve answered. "I have half a mind to shoot you myself."

Steve felt as though he was being messed with, but it was hard to just block out the emotion he had inside for this person who he had loved and respected just short days before.

"Stevie, you are not a killer. I tried to make you a killer but you are not. Just like Yuri. I used to think people like you are weak, but you aren't. I want to ask you, as a friend, let me jump off that cliff I was running towards. It is not more than a hundred yards. You can watch me. My time is over; your time- your life is just beginning."

"Turn the fuck around and start back to where we came from. I don't believe you, Molnar or Kevlov or whoever the fuck you are."

Kevlov started to walk closer, moving towards the gun.

"Don't make me do this," Steve said. "I don't want to kill you, but I will." Steve began to shake.

"It will be easy, Stevie. Just let me...." BANG!!! Steve fired the gun, almost without realizing it. The bullet entered Kevlov's heart, and he fell to the ground, seemingly smiling his grin, his evil grin, laughing from beyond the grave.

In a few minutes, Control caught up with them. He had borrowed the cop's gun and went ahead to help Steve. "Son," he told Steve, "You're a brave one. This man is one of the most dangerous killers I've ever known. I'll see you get rewarded for this. I spoke with the Constable back there; he said you want to leave town. We'll make sure you and your family are set up wherever you want. Vancouver is as good a place as any. Just one thing."

"What's that?"

"You didn't see me, you didn't know me, and, if anyone ever asks, you didn't do this. It's hard to kill a man, I know, but walk yourself into a church, pray to God and confess, and leave it there and go on with your life. I'll have someone out there counsel you for all this bullshit you've been through, and it will be all confidential. Get me?"

"I think I understand." And with that, Steve uncocked the action on the gun, handed it back to Control and as he looked at Kevlov's body, with the life force gone from it, he took a deep breath. He wondered how he was going to face Lisa, if she called him tomorrow.

Chapter Eleven

Steve never even had a chance to go back to the trailer. He was flown to Victoria, where his parents and Colin met up with him, and they left everything behind. They vacationed there for two glorious weeks, and when they were done, they weren't taken back to Walker Lake, but they were taken to a house in Vancouver's west end that must have cost more than all of them together would make in a lifetime. Steve's Dad was given a supervisory job with a construction company that paid enough to keep the family going and Steve was given enough to start his business, actually more than enough to do so and be comfortable for a while, which made all the Hansens happy.

The hardest thing Steve had to do was to get to the counselor that Control had set him up with, and talk things out. One time, when he went to see the counselor, he was told something that seemed to make a small change in him. The psychologist told him that even though he was strong and caring and wanted to, he didn't have to help everyone he knew through everything that happened. Steve had told her about Colin falling through the ice and, after a lot of reassurances that everything he said was confidential, he talked about Lisa being hurt, and the strong drive in him to make sure that Sean would be unable to hurt anyone else. It seemed that all of his life, he had been trying to be Superman, when Superman was really just an idea of a perfect person that doesn't exist.

After a few weeks of daily trips to his psychologist, Steve genuinely started to feel better. At first he had tried to be tough and said that the thought of losing Lisa didn't scare him, but then as time went by, he started to talk about her more. One day, he started to realize that Lisa was a woman who loved him and who his family loved, but somehow he had wanted to punish himself for not being there for her when she got hurt, and so, he tried to take all the good Lisa had brought to him and throw it away. Now this was something he no longer wanted to do.

He was going to still need to get counseling for some time, but he was starting to feel more ready to 'go home,' so to speak. There was just one more thing that Control had suggested that he was going to do.

The age-stained Catholic church, not far from downtown, was an easy walk from the psychologist's office. Steve had never gone to church much, and didn't really know any of the traditions or protocols for praying, but he had been past this building many times. There was something about the artistry and the reverence to God in how it looked to him; that this was where he really wanted to go and pour out his soul.

He arrived at the church around 2:00p.m., and, finding the door open, and the great high ceilings and beautiful stained glass and statues comforting, he went in and felt a strong feeling of peace come over him. He walked down the centre isle, took a random seat, folded down a kneeling bar and started to pray. He went on and on, opening himself up about how he wanted to help raise Colin, and how he loved his family, and all the things he had done. He cried a little, thinking of all the shit he had been through, and when he could say no more, he leaned back to discover that there was a robed man sitting next to him. This nearly scared him to death, most of what he said he had been told, never to repeat, so he talked to the priest-like figure.

"Are you a priest?" was his first question.

"Yes I am. My name is Father Anthony," came the reply.

"Did you overhear what I said?"

"Yes I did, son, just a little of it. I just wanted to come and explain to you, that we all have sinned and fallen short of the glory of God, but when we reach out to Him and show him we feel guilty, especially when we end up doing the right thing, He will always take us back in His arms and forgive us."

"Can I confess my sins to you, Father?"

"I'm sorry, son. Confession is a sacrament of the Catholic faith. Are you Catholic?"

"No, but I want to be. I want to raise my family to know that God protects us, just like you said."

"This is no small decision. We have a class you can attend in the fall, but the last thing we want to do, is have you change your mind later. Go and discuss this with your family, and come back when you are sure. I will pray with you now and your sins will be forgiven, I promise you."

"Father...umm..."

"Are you worried I won't be able to keep your secrets?"

"Kind of."

"You don't have to worry. Priests are sworn to secrecy when they minister, plus..." The priest took off his dark glasses to reveal that he had no eyes.

"How did that happen, Father?"

"When I was a young and foolish priest, I tried to talk a friend into not getting an abortion and her boyfriend took out his frustrations on me. I have forgiven him, and now God has opened up new ways for me to serve the church." Steve felt incredibly humbled. He prayed with the father, took some information about the program to join the church, and walked home in silence.

It was a rainy day when Steve decided it would be safe to visit Lisa.

He arrived at her apartment and knocked at her door. His beautiful former girlfriend answered the door in her bathrobe, looking pretty tired. "Steve! Oh my God, I've been so worried about you! Why didn't you let me know you were alright?"

"I wanted to. Believe me I did, but we were told to be very careful. I can't say too much, but things ended up alright. I helped the police out with something and I got a reward." Lisa looked into his eyes and didn't like what she saw.

"Helped? You didn't...you didn't kill Sean, did you?"

"I didn't kill Sean. I had a hell of a rough time though, and I'm seeing someone about it. I'm a mess Lisa, and I need you." Lisa began to cry and pulled Steve close to her.

"I need you too, Stevie, I need you so much. I've never loved anyone like you. I'm so glad you got help."

"I did get help. But I can't ever imagine living life without you. Lisa...?"
"Yes?"
"Will you marry me and stay by my side, forever?"
"I will Stevie, I will. I just want you to know that..."
"That what?"

"I want you to know that I went and got a second opinion. They said with time, with healing, and a possible operation, there is actually a very good chance of me getting pregnant again, and having a normal, healthy baby."

"Oh my God, babe. That's so awesome!"
"We can even start trying now, if you like."
"Yeah, I think I would like that. I think I would like that a lot."

With that simple understanding, that he was to be her only forevermore, and she was to be his as well, to the day they died. They made their embrace and each touching of skin, cheek to cheek, mouth to lips, and body to body, the most beautiful and electrifying experience either had ever known. They moved in to embrace each other and seemed as one as they hurriedly locked the door, and Lisa slipped out of her robe. As Steve moved close to her, he swore to himself that he had never seen or imagined a female body that could be so beautiful. He reached out to hold her head and moved close to her for a deep, wet, slow, passionate kiss and felt her slim, but curvaceous figure naked against him. Within moments, he was naked, as well, and she liked how fit and muscular he had become, even more so than, just a few months before. He lifted her up in his strong arms, kissing her neck and cheek and behind her ears. There was just no way anything could have been more perfect for the young couple. This was what he had hoped would come back to him, not just the lovemaking, but the symbiosis, the feeling of two becoming one. He laid her down on her bed and in the dim light of the rainy sky, he made passion-filled love to her, until they both were exhausted. It was perfection; it was so much more than what he thought would become of his life, just those few weeks ago.

Steve and Lisa married on a sunny summer day, in a small, private outdoor wedding in the shadow of the Rocky Mountains, not far from the city. After a year or two, showing tourists what Canada was all about, Steve grew to love Vancouver and, not too long after that, he grew to love his and Lisa's two children even more.

THE END

When Some Come Marching Home

Two brothers and their mother sat around the kitchen table of the modest Victorian home the boys had lived in their whole lives. The fare was sparse: rationing had been in place now for some time, but, in a way, it was good for them. People living in a time without rationing would likely be overweight and unhealthy compared to most. The two boys, one in the twelfth grade and the other in the eleventh, spent their summers working on their Uncle's farm for long hours and little pay. The hard work made them fit and the sports and activities that young people enjoyed in those days kept them that way. It was expected they would work on the farm because labor workers were hard to come by. Most of the men who could pull their own weight had gone off to fight the war in Europe and the slack had to be taken up somehow.

Two years before the unimaginable had happened, they had gotten notice that their father had died fighting the Kaiser. Perhaps the boys were too young to understand how important their father was to their mother and their own lives and, though there was mourning for nearly a year, they seemed to have bounced back. Their mother hadn't, and all she dreamed about was the war ending before her boys had to go, before she had to say goodbye forever to another of her loved ones.

"Hey, Mom!" Eric, the older of the two boys started to say, as he looked down with distaste at the boiled vegetables the boy's mother had put on their plates to round out the tiny ration of meat. "Our teacher was telling us about this battle called Vimy Ridge. He was there."

"How could he have been there and have come back?" Jimmy, the younger of the two spat out sounding judgmental, as though Eric's teacher had 'dropped the ball' as it were and came home a coward.

“Hey, give him a break! He lost his leg in that battle!” Eric snapped back.

“Go ahead with what you wanted to say, Eric, and Jimmy, don't interrupt.”

“Okay,” Eric replied and began again. “Well, he was in this battle called Vimy Ridge and he said it was mostly Canadians in the fight. They had tunnels and mines and superior artillery and all the men had been specially trained for this one battle. He said when all was said and done the Canadians had handed the British their first victory of the war. And he said now that the Americans are in things we just might be able to get those lousy Germans for good.”

“Eric, it's good you love your country, and I can't stop you from learning about the war, but I want you to know there is nothing glorious about that place. Millions of people have died out there, I talked to Mr. Westmore about it. He wasn't so lucky. He can't even walk. His feet rotted right off his legs. He said you stand knee deep in water and mud and the pounding from the enemy guns never stops. He said men go insane from the sound and, if they won't fight, they shoot them. I lost your father. I don't want to lose you for some far off British war that makes no sense." As she said this, she tried to hide her tears, but the boys could see them. Eric felt sad too and had to hold back a tear or two as he remembered how kind and caring his father had been when he wasn't drinking or working himself to death trying to make ends meet.

"Nice work, Eric!" Jim said as he smacked his brother in the back of the head. "You made her cry. Don't you have any feelings?"

"Watch it half-pint or you'll be crying yourself in no time." Eric answered.

"Both of you boys go to your rooms and study and do your homework. You have no idea how lucky you both are that you have school to go to and a house to come home to. It wasn't so wonderful here when we first got to this place. Your father had to work so hard! Now get-get!"

"Okay, Mom. We'll get down to it." Eric said, and gave his brother an equal smack to the one he received once they were out of sight.

It took Eric about two hours to finish up all his work. He hated every minute of it: going through all these math equations and writing an essay about Wolfe and Montcalm and their battle for control of Canada. When he was done, he peeked into his brother's room and when he saw Jim was lying back and throwing a ball, he knew it was the best time to talk to him. He went back to his own room for a minute and got his baseball glove. Then he walked to Jim's room, opened the door and threw the glove onto his brother's stomach.

"What's this all about?" Jim asked.

"I want you to have that. I know you always wanted one and I guess now it will fit you, so it's yours." Eric replied.

"Well, of course I want one, but what are you going to use when we play ball out at the farm this summer?"

"I won't be going to the farm with you."

"Does that mean you're going to...?"

"Yes, as soon as I write my last exam next week I'm signing up. Couple of guys from school and I are going together. That means you have to stay here and take care of Mom."

“But why? Why would you go off to Europe if you didn't have to?” Jim asked.

“Because I just don't think it's right that Pa had to die for us and I won't get a shot at those Germans for what they did. Everyone's in this fight. It's not just a British War. We're British, too, in a way. If I don't go I'll regret it for the rest of my days.”

“Can I go with you?” Jim said sympathetically.

“Absolutely not. They won't take you at your age anyway, not without Mom signing for you. She won't do that and, besides, you need to stay and help out. Understand?” Eric replied sternly.

“Understood.”

“Then the glove is yours. After I'm gone you can have my comics and my Sherlock Holmes collection and anything else you want. I won't be needing them.”

“Why would you say that Eric? You'll come back!”

“Well, do what you like with them. If you want to read the stuff, read it and when I come back you can give it back to me, but

I figure I won't be much interested in comics after I go to war. Okay?"

"Yeah, okay."

Just like he said, in a week, Eric was gone. His Mother cried for a few days after reading the note he left, but in some small way she was proud of him. She knew it wasn't right to keep him there but it hurt her deeply. Somewhere in the back of her mind she knew he would come home. He was a smart boy, just not in school things. He would make it.

Eric and his friends finished up their exams and then headed down to the Prince of Wales armoury without even saying goodbye and signed themselves up for the Royal Canadian Army. There weren't many questions asked of them. They assumed it was because they needed a lot of men. One of his friends was stopped and asked if he were old enough, and after he produced his birth certificate they let him move on. They spent the rest of the day being told the rudiments of marching and were given uniforms and then did a lot of waiting.

The next day they marched all the recruits they had gathered off to a train station and were herded aboard a train headed for Eastern Canada. Most of the boys and men in the group had never been outside of Edmonton, and a lot of the younger boys had never been away from their families. The Prairie scenery was green and beautiful, but, as Eric looked around, there weren't an awful lot of dry eyes in the crowd.

When they arrived at their training camp, everyone was soon kept far too busy for tears, except for the hour given them at the end of the day to write letters or catch up on their rest. A tough Sergeant with battle scars on his face was the closest thing to a parent they had, and he was often not a very nice one.

"You men," The Sergeant addressed them on the first day, "are the soldiers of the King. Every one of you has made an oath to serve King and Country and I am going to tell you that is just what you will do. You men will not fail to do this because anyone who does will cease to exist. Have any of you seen an officer yet? Raise your hands." A few men put up their hands. "Our Royal Canadian officers, who you will only address as 'Sir' and salute as you walk by, have an interesting bit of fashion built into their uniforms. You see, their pistols are at the end of a lanyard that goes around their shoulders. Does anyone know what this lanyard is for?" One man put up his hand. "Yes, you there. Can you tell us what the lanyard is for?"

"It's so they don't lose it if they're riding a horse or fall in a battle."

"It is used for that, so they don't lose it, very good. But the lanyard also serves another purpose. You see, the officer's lanyard doesn't let him aim the pistol very well, if it did, someone could get the pistol from him and use it on him. The lanyard is short, which means it is there for the officer to shoot his own men from the hip if they get out of hand. I want to tell you men that you are all very brave to join up, but I also want you to know that the second you step out of line you will be dealt with. That is your first lesson about the army. Don't let it be your last. When you signed up, you signed your life away, so be ready to give it so those left behind don't have to." Some of the men glanced at the others and all of them could see a sinking feeling was setting in the general mood of the group.

Not much more than three days later, a new flood of

recruits came in. While this was happening, Eric was at lunch in the battalion mess hall and as he came out his heart sank. There was Jim, his little Jimmy who he had tried to protect and fight for all his life, who was just barely 16, standing before him smiling, in the uniform of a Canadian Soldier.

"Hey, Brother!" Jim said to Eric.

"What the hell are you doing? I thought we talked about this! How did you get by the recruiters?" Eric said, blindsided by the thought that he was going to have to worry about his brother and mother now until the war had ended.

"Relax, Eric! I used Joey Miner's birth certificate. I figured you were right. I had to go to this war or I would regret it forever." Jimmy said, not realizing that he had broken his mother's heart.

"You're coming with me. I'm turning you in, Jimmy."

"You want me to go to jail? Come on, be a sport. I'm family, remember?"

"Of course I remember. Of course I can't get you sent to jail. Fuck! Do you know what you've done?"

“I made a decision, Eric, for the first time in my life I made my own decision about something important.” Jim said.

“Well, brother, I'm going to keep my eyes on you. You're not going to do anything stupid or say anything stupid and maybe if we keep both of our sets of eyes on each other we'll get through this.” Eric replied, the emotion on his face looking anything but happy.

As the next few weeks went by, they were given rifles, Lee Enfield .303 rifles and they learned to clean them, to shoot with them, to march with them and even sleep with them. They were given lesson after lesson in everything from hygiene to marksmanship and even a lecture or two on the dangers of the French 'working women' and how to prevent social diseases. It seemed like forever, but eventually they were shipped out in a huge transport convoy across the pond. It all seemed so celebratory when they left the docks. There was an army band playing. People and soldiers were waving the Union Jack. A general air of invincibility was about them. When they were too far to see the shore, it took little time for the waving and happy soldiers to take their rum rations and playing cards and dice and laugh and gamble the day away. Eric would have nothing of either, and after numerous letters full of promises to their Mom, he made sure Jim didn't either.

Two days into their voyage to England, Eric was woken by a sound he hadn't heard since he was a kid blowing up stumps, clearing land on his Uncle's farm. There was a rush to get topside, and when he did he saw one of the other troop ships taking on water and dozens of men jumping and diving off the side, some others trying to get lifeboats out and failing because of the press of the crowds onboard. Before too much longer, another ship was hit by torpedo and the carnage began again. The first ship that had been hit had now rolled on its back and the few men that could had scrambled to stay on top or find wreckage to cling to, or, sadly, drown. There was little that could be done because few of the troop ships were armed, and even if they were, the priority would be to stop the enemy before saving the drowning men.

After the second hit, a destroyer that had been escorting them gave chase to the German submarine which, when it saw the destroyer coming, had dived underwater. The destroyer moved in and started dropping depth charges, and, seemingly, after a thousand of them had been loosed, wreckage and the grim sight of drowned men came up to the surface. The men on the troop ships cheered and yelled, waving their thanks to the fighting ship, and finally were able to begin to pull men from the water. Eric learned later that over a thousand Canadians, many of whom he had known and trained with, had perished in the open sea. Despite this, since the submarine had been destroyed, they still felt as though they were invincible and that in the grim face of war that honorable victory was possible.

Eric and Jim's days in England were incredible. Off in most of the country, where rationing and loss of sons and fathers had devastated the will of the people, it was not so, but in London, where the brothers were allowed to spend a short leave, people saw the Canadians and the Americans who were starting to come over as saviors who were to be wined and dined and treated like kings. The girls were willing and friendly, the scotch flowed freely, and, though it was just to last a couple of days, the festivities, formal and informal were just about enough to make men forget.

When their leave was done, once again, the Canadians that Eric and James were trained with, were loaded on transports and shipped to France, where they were stuffed into trains and sent off all over the front, wherever replacements were needed. For the next seven months, though they were fortunate to be together, the brothers endured worse conditions than they ever could have imagined. One day a barrage would come down, from the German lines and it would last for days, the shells blasting and booming and exploding in willy-nilly fashion. Their British commanders tried to make the trenches in short breaks and tight angles so one shell wouldn't kill a hundred men or more, but the shells killed enough. One of the worst things about the enemy artillery was that it made shell holes that would be followed by rain, and as one was trying to get to anywhere there was always the chance of slipping in the mire and falling into one of these holes where you could easily drown. All the mud and wet would often get into men's boots and their socks would rot on their feet.

Once, Eric was standing watch, poking his head slightly out of the top of the trench, looking for raiding parties who might want information of the Canadian/British strength, and he heard a man screaming his lungs out from a dugout below. As the screaming began, a huge rat came running out of the same dugout with something in his mouth and then the man who was screaming came next.

"My toe! That fucking rat has got my toe!" He was screaming. Apparently his foot had become so rotten from trench foot that a rat had been able to snap off a little snack for himself. Though it may have been the darkest humour he had ever encountered, Eric laughed to himself and when he re-told the story later many men found it funny. The conditions were so bad that you had to laugh at these sick things or you would go crazy wondering when it would happen to you.

Eric and James had been in a few German attacks, as horrible as the sounds and sights of shelling was, when shelling stopped, you knew the enemy was going to try and hit you and hit you hard. It was during attacks that the most gruesome sights would be witnessed. During the shelling, the British would set up machine gun emplacements, and when the attack came, Germans would come running or even walking and would get mowed down in row after bleeding screaming row. Sometimes attacks or feint attacks would come at night and someone would fire of a flare and for a few seconds you would see these men coming, looking more sinister and bloodthirsty as the devil himself and the machine guns and artillery would go off then the flare would fizzle out and for a few terrifying seconds nothing could be seen but the muzzle flashes of the enemy rifles. The men in the trenches would fire their bolt-action .303's, but the highest death toll always came from the machine guns. Sometimes a German or two would make it to the British trench and a bevy of men angered by the shelling, angered by the war would take out whatever they could on these men, stabbing and kicking them repeatedly with their bayonets and boots until they were a bloody pulp. After a while, there would be blood and mud in the trenches and in the shell craters and everything seemed to be that crimson red that flowed from men whether they were German or British or Canadian. Most people were never the same after seeing such things. Even the newest of the new recruits were old men when they had been through a day or two like that.

By some strange luck, the two brothers were never in a full-scale assault against the Germans. This was where the real blood-letting of the 'good guys' would happen. Though Vimy was highly different, where each man had been highly knowledgeable of their objectives and everything was co-ordinated down to the very second, most of the attacks were planned and carried out by men who cared little for the lives and well-being of their troops. It didn't matter that men would go home without limbs or the use of their eyes, sent home blind to sit out the rest of their days in darkness. It didn't matter that a thousand or ten thousand Canadians all from the same city would be piled into mass graves of war dead. What mattered to the leaders was that they could prove to their superiors that attacks were indeed being made. Had the British stayed simply on the defensive and repelled attacks they could have easily sweated out the Germans, but politics and the complaints of their allies made things different.

Eric and James had been on raiding and reconnaissance parties that brought them over to enemy lines at night, and had made something of a name for themselves. Some of these enemy position stalking sessions were a lot like times back home when the two brothers were off to supplement their meat rations with a little deer or rabbit. These raiding parties were extremely dangerous and, yet, time and again the two would head out into no-man's land to mark out positions for further artillery attacks on the enemy or other assaults. After five months in France, Eric had become a Sergeant and James a Corporal from the merit their superiors saw they deserved. During one of these raids, Eric was shot in the shoulder and the bullet was lodged in him. He was sent back and had the bad luck of not being near one of the portable x-ray machines that had helped save so many lives. The shell was in him and it had to come out but the Doctor had no idea where it was, so he had to use the old method to find it. This method was a bit grotesque and messy. The surgeon had to take his scalpel and stab it into the man's flesh and put it in deep enough so he could tell whether or not the bullet was in that particular position. What got messy was sometimes you would get a surgeon who was a rotten guesser like Eric did and when he came out of the hospital he had 15 stab wounds in his shoulder which would never be the same. He was able to still fire his rifle with accuracy, though, so he was sent back to the front.

One day late in October of 1918, some shuffling of troops went on in the front lines. Eric and James were pulled out of their relatively safe position and replaced by a large number of American troops. There was something going on within the British

High Command, and Eric had been briefed on it, but as James was just a Corporal, Eric was forbidden to share the news with him. The two were getting worn down. Eric had constant pain from his wound and was starting to get terrible nightmares, but his spirits were high. There was a feeling about the trenches that things were coming to a close. Rumors went up and down the lines that the Germans were in trouble, that the Americans had brought in so many men the war was now within reach of being over.

"Eric," James said to his brother and leader one day. "What's going on? You don't talk much to me anymore."

"Nothing to talk about really. You hear the rumors. This war is going to be done with."

"Yeah, but there are other rumors. Like now that Germany doesn't have to fight in the East they have a lot more men. And there are rumors that they're going to mass for a huge attack right along this front. What do you say about that?" James replied, sounding a bit angry.

"I can't tell you anything you know that. I'm sworn to secrecy. The kind of secrecy that gets you killed if you break it. Treason, get it? I can't say, and damn you for asking me."

"My own brother knows we're going to die and he won't say anything."

James sneered at Eric with a mean and vengeful look about him, then walked off, his feet slapping the layer of water that covered the bottom of the trench. James didn't let on, but he was near his breaking point. He had come this far and he couldn't see any way out of what was going to happen in the next few days, which he was sure would be an attack he would never survive. He hadn't told anyone but trench foot had set in both of his feet as well and it looked so bad and seemed so painful that he felt for sure the doctors would have to amputate. He didn't want to go home a cripple and he couldn't face the idea of being over-run by a million screaming Germans. He went into his cramped dugout, picked up the Luger he had picked off a dead German in a raid and pointed it to his head. He sat for a few minutes, thought about the life he once had, when he had a mother and a father and hot summer nights with pretty girls from around the farm, weekends in the fresh air hunting and exploring. He thought about all this and how it was never to be again and then he pulled the trigger and splattered his brains against the wall of his dugout. In a few minutes, Eric came in with a piece of paper he had gotten from the Captain of their unit which gave him permission to reveal the secret he had kept from James. The war was over. The Germans had surrendered, and the paper was instructions on how to process all the prisoners they would be taking. Victory was theirs. But victory was not for James. At least not now.

When Eric saw his younger brother sitting there lifeless something snapped. He just sat down. Sitting down in that dugout was perhaps the last thing he ever did as his own free will. He was alive, but he never moved again of his own free will. He was shipped back to Edmonton, to a newly built hospital for the mentally ill which had been built for men like him. Men who never stopped screaming. Men who heard shells fall around them. Men who were very far from any concept of reality that you or I may conceive of. For the next 18 years, Eric lived he sat in that hospital in a comatose state, someone changing his diapers, wiping the drool from his mouth and spoon feeding him. Inside all his brain knew was dreams, dreams. Just like the ones his brother had in 1918. Summer days and happy winter evenings. Sledding parties that never ended.

All anyone else could see was his hollow stare that men got when they went 'over there' and never really came back.

The Odd Story of George The Barber

It was a hot and dry midsummer day in the small Alberta town of Westlock. Just off Main Street, there was a barber trying to beat the heat out in front of his shop by sitting in the shade and sipping an icy cold pop. Above him a sign proudly displayed, "Barber Shop, Established 1975." Old George, as people had taken to calling him lately, always had a story or a joke to tell with each cut. Everyone knew that George had come up from the US in the early 70's as a draft dodger, and really had no intention of going back. Like many of the people in Westlock, he liked being known by everyone he saw each day and how quiet the town was. Most younger people went to the big city at about 18 or 19 and soon grew tired of it and ended up back here.

On this particular afternoon, there hadn't been too many customers aside from a couple of young men in their 20's, so George was glad when he saw one of the town's RCMP officers walking towards his shop. These guys always got their hair trimmed and didn't fuss much and of course always paid up front rather than asking for an extension to the end of the month as some did. As he drew closer George could see it was Constable Murray who was coming. He looked kind of serious but then most cops always looked serious.

"Howdy, George!" Constable Ralph Murray said.

"Well, hey there, young fellah! I can see you're getting a bit shaggy under your hat there. Come right in and sit down. Tell me your troubles." George replied.

"Well, before I sit down I wanted to ask you a couple of questions first. Have you heard of those two brothers went by the name Murphy?"

"Murphy. Murphy. Knew a Murphy family used to drive up here from St.Albert for some kind of Mormon meetings. Haven't seen them in quite a few years." George said, squinting a bit from the sun.

"No, these two boys were from Vimy. Their Mother called our detachment and said they were late coming home and that they knew she needed their help on the farm, said it wasn't like them at all to not show up for chores. I've asked around a bit and someone said they directed them up to see you for a haircut."

"Oh, okay. I did give a couple of cuts to two boys, just over 20 I would guess. They sat still, paid and went on their way. What makes you come here to ask?"

"Well, I know you can get to talking and I thought maybe they told you where they were headed." The Constable explained.

"We just mostly talked about baseball. Can you believe those boys didn't think the Blue Jays had a chance this year?" George said as he laughed to himself in a bit of a strange fashion. The Constable chuckled back.

"George, just because the Blue Jays won a couple of World Series' back in the 90's doesn't mean they're the best in the League still. Now can you give me a quick cut or can't you?"

"Sure can, Ralph, step inside." George said.

George dusted off his only barber chair, dipped his combs and clippers in alcohol and took a sheet and shook it out and covered up the Constable's uniform with a flourish worthy of a bullfighter. As he tied off the neck, his customer said, "Oh and can I get a shave, too? Being blonde is nice. You don't have to shave much, but I get lazy sometimes. Haven't shaved in three days, if my superior saw that he would transfer me to the Northwest Territories." Bill said with a laugh.

George looked at the straight razor he kept and a tight feeling went through his stomach. He picked it up and ran it across a leather strop to sharpen it and he could see his hand tremble. He knew what had to be done.

"I'll be right back, Ralph. I just need some more shaving cream." George lied, taking the half-full can he already had sitting back with him. He ducked down in the back and took the Mickey bottle he kept there and had a good swig. He was glad that this would take away his shakes by the time the cut was finished and he would be able to do the shave.

"Hey, George!" Ralph yelled, making the aging barber jump and bang his head on a shelf.

"Fuck fuck fuck!" Ralph said quietly to himself as a couple of drops of blood fell on the floor.

"What's that, George?" The Constable asked.

"Oh nothing. What can I do for you?" George replied

"Can you put on the radio for me? I want to hear if there is any word about those boys."

"Sure thing. I'll be right out." George replied before taking one last quick swig.

George came out from the back with the old can of shaving cream and set it down, rubbed the sore spot on his head and put the radio on. It was an ancient set and you could hear it crackle as he tuned it in. For a moment it stopped on a Johnny Cash song about a prison and George hummed along with it for a little while, then realized he was looking for news and switched stations to an all news station.

"How's that, Ralph?" George asked.

"Oh, just fine. I wouldn't mind listening to Johnny Cash to be honest, but work is work." Came the reply.

"I can side with you there, my friend." George said.

The haircut went well but the Constable could tell that George was nervous, shaky. Everyone knew George liked to drink a bit, but this didn't seem normal. Over the past ten years or so that Ralph had been working in Westlock, there had been a couple of missing person cases here and there that never seemed to get solved. Mostly they were drug related. Some people had mentioned and he had heard from some of his own sources that Westlock was pretty bad for drugs. When these missing person cases came up, Ralph and his fellow officers would team up with a few other detachments in the area and round up all persons of interest, but it always seemed like they had rock-solid alibi's. Not only that but none of them even seemed like they had committed a crime. Then here, the only person that no one in the world could suspect seemed to have something to hide. George finished up the haircut and mixed up some shaving cream and started in on the shave. His shaking had slowed, but, all of a sudden, Ralph jumped up like his life depended on it. He saw blood all over George's hand and it scared the shit out of him.

"What's the matter for heaven's sake, Ralph? I didn't cut you!" George exclaimed.

"I know, but what the hell is that blood for?" Constable Murray yelled, pointing at George's hand, then looking at the floor, "And that blood, leading to the back! What the hell you got going on here, George?"

"Nothing, nothing at all for heaven's sake!" He yelled back. "I banged my head on that shelf and it bled a bit."

"Then why the hell were you all shaky when you gave me that cut?"

"Because I was in pain for gosh-darned it! I told you-I smacked my head. And well...."

"Well what? George, if you want me to help you, you have to be honest with me." Ralph said, starting to calm his tone of voice.

George buried his hands in his face and said, "I'm getting old. Getting old and drinking too much. One of these days not too long from now I'm going to have to close up shop, and I don't know what the hell I'm going to do. I found out I can go back to California and stay with my sister, but I don't even have the damn money to get there on the bus!" Ralph could see tears were running down the poor old guy's face.

"George, you've been my friend for all the ten years I've been here and you've got a lot more friends you knew even longer. I can help you if you're telling me the truth. Trouble is, my gut tells me that I have to check this out. I don't know what's going on here, I can't be sure someone isn't forcing you into something. There's been a lot of bad stuff going on and we have to follow every lead. I want you to stay here while I go get a search warrant. I'm going to call in one of my men to watch you, make sure nothing funny goes on while I get it. Can you understand that? After we clear you we'll see what we can do about that bus ticket."

George's eyes seemed to glow again, partly in happiness and partly in relief. Ralph got on his portable radio, called in a car and watched George as he sat in his hot shop listening to the radio and sullenly drinking a pop. A couple of hours later Ralph came back.

"Okay George, I want you to know your rights. This here is a search warrant. It's been signed here by a judge. It says I can look through your shop here, go through your receipts. I see you don't have a video camera so that part doesn't matter. I can look anywhere, and if I find anything beyond a slip of paper for a baseball pool I'm going to have to arrest you. Do you understand that, George?"

"Yes, I'm pretty sure I understand that all."

George replied, looking a bit helpless.

"Okay, first, what's under your counter there?" The Constable said, pointing to the cupboards under the mirror. George opened it for him. There were a lot of empty bottles of rye, only the cheapest brands. If Ralph thought this was odd he didn't let on.

"And this blood. You say it's yours?" He said, pointing to the trail of blood that came from the back.

"Yes, of course. Here, you can see where I hit the shelf on my head and you can see the spot on my head that was bleeding." George answered.

"Okay, that sounds fine. Now, what's behind this door?" Ralph asked, pointing to a door near the back that didn't lead outside.

"That's for storage. It leads down to the basement. I keep stuff I don't use much in it. I don't like clutter around my apartment." George replied.

"I'm going to have to look down there. Is there a light or window?"

"There's a light but you'll also need this flashlight." George said, handing him a flashlight, feeling angry, feeling betrayed. Part of him wanted to give his so-called 'friend' a kick that would send him down the stairs. Maybe from now on he would give cops the worst haircuts until they try going to Edmonton for theirs

"Not much down here." Ralph said after he got to the bottom. "Boxes, dirt floor, broken lamp. You should have a garage sale George, some of this stuff might sell."

"And have some jerks pay me 10cents for things I saved for years to buy? No, not worth it. Better to have memories. Better to have something to show for all these years." George answered, sounding sad.

"Well George, I'm satisfied, you're not hiding two boys down here. Funny thing though, I talked to those boy's mothers and she said they most likely headed North after getting a cut. She said it sounded like them to take off like that. They had talked for a while about being big-shots after working in the oilfields for a while. She just never thought they would get off their lazy asses and do it. So we're going to close the case anyhow."

"Well, that's good to know. Be a terrible thing for two boys to break their mother's heart like that, but that's what kids are like these days. Maybe you're right. Maybe I should sell some stuff and head to Sacramento with the proceeds. I'll miss this town, but there is always a time to go."

"Well, you know what? I talked to my co-workers and they didn't think the cost of a ticket to the US should be out of your reach after the years you've served this community. We put together a little cash for a ticket and some sandwiches on the way. We can even sell your stuff for you if you want to leave sooner and send you the money. There's a bus headed for Calgary three or four times a day from Edmonton, and once you get there you can buy another ticket for the States. Here, it's all in this envelope." Ralph took out an envelope that had been folded in half from his shirt pocket and handed it over, giving George a pat on the shoulder and a smile.

"Ralph, Ralphy. This is the nicest thing anyone has done for me. You're a good kid, you know. You always were a good kid. I think I'm going to close up, buy a ticket then go home and pack and call my sister. This is really going to be something. Thank you so very much, and thank you to all your friends. I'll write to you when I get to Sacramento and let you know where to send the money. And you make sure the cost of this ticket comes out of it!"

"You've got it, George. We're all going to miss you, so send us a card now and then, okay?" Ralph said, feeling a bit teary-eyed. They hugged and said no more, George sat down, counted out his money, plus what he kept in the till, wrote out a couple of letters and walked down to the post office to mail them, then went back to close up his shop for good.

When he was done, just two hours before the Edmonton bus was to leave Westlock, George took out his keys and opened up the door to his basement one last time. He picked up a pry bar and after sweeping away some dirt that was around three inches deep, he used the pry bar to lift a steel cover he had placed over a hole in the dirt floor of the basement. At the bottom of the hole were the two Murphy brothers. First he took a picture of the corpses, then George went to a box marked Hydrochloric Acid, took out two gallon jugs and poured it over the bodies as they dissolved into nothing. How many times he had done this he didn't know, but it was old hat now. He waited until the bodies and the acid had mostly gone, covered up the hole with the plate again, spread dirt over the hole, then went home to pack.

George filled two suitcases with clothes and a few books and from a closet gun safe he took out a photo album. On the way there, he stopped at a store where you can print pictures by yourself on a coin-operated machine. When he got to the Bus Stop he checked in his suitcases and took his photo album on the bus. The wheat fields and forests slid past him as he looked through the pages of his book. So many newspaper clippings, so many faces. He got to the very last page of his scrapbook where there was already something written, but no picture. He slid in the instant picture into the space, then read the caption to himself. It said: "Murphy boys, came to visit a neighbor 1989, broke my apartment window with a baseball, couldn't replace the screen and dealt with mosquitos all that summer. He wrote in, Murphy boys, 2010, dealt with.

George got off the bus in Edmonton, then transferred to a Vancouver bus. It was a long ride but it was worth it to see the mountains. He got off in a place called Kamloops, found a barber who was hiring and never left until the day he died, two years later.

Zack and the Rabbit

Zack never took the killing part of hunting too seriously, he thought to himself as he stepped gently on the leaves, branches and roots on the path he was walking on. He liked the idea that he was improving his aim and developing a skill that one day may come in handy, especially if he joined the Armed Forces one day when he was older, like he had wanted to ever since he watched his first war movie as a kid. People who knew how to shoot in that line of work advanced quickly to things like sniper school and Special Forces training. If it meant the life of the odd tiny bird or squirrel then so be it. He even had biblical evidence that there was nothing wrong with what he did, or so he thought since he had never read the Bible in his life. He had heard, though, that right in the first page of the Bible it said that mankind could do whatever it wanted with all the other animals on Earth.

There was, of course, also the enjoyment Zack got just from being outdoors, but when he was hunting there was something else, another kind of thrill. It had to be the feeling he used to get playing wide games of 'capture the flag' when he was younger. He remembered running down a guy who was a couple years younger than him and a couple or more pounds heavier than him. The adrenalin rush that came from chasing down a person, tackling them and taking their flag was so incredible he had decided right then and there he would one day be a soldier.

As he stood on the brink of manhood, the feeling was the same, but now the game was a lot more real. He had taken a step up from the game to the point where he had a real rifle and could actually kill. The next step, of course, would be when he was in the Army and then, of course, he would be in the situation of 'kill or be killed.' He was learning bit by bit how to make note of the wind direction and how to step on the forest floor without making noise. He learned how to sneak up to small birds and to listen to every sound around him so he was ready if something he could shoot at reared its head.

As he was walking at this particular moment, he heard a bit of scuffling near a clearing up ahead. Stealthily and slowly he walked towards the sound and had his .22 rifle at the ready and his eyes peeled for movement. As he drew closer to where the sound came from, a jack rabbit jumped out of a bush and tried to make its way across the clearing when bang! A clear and well-aimed shot rang out that would mean the end of the poor beautiful creature's life.

“Shit shit shit! I got a rabbit! Man, I have never gotten a rabbit!” Zack exclaimed though no one was around to hear him.

He walked up to the creature and saw that he was bleeding but still breathing. Zack recycled the bolt on his rifle and put one last shot into the rabbit's head to kill him. After that, he really didn't know what to do. He had no means of carrying the bleeding carcass. He didn't have a knife with him to skin it, either. He just kind of rolled the dead thing over and looked at it. Then, as the sun was going down, he just left the scene of the killing and headed back to his car.

That night, Zack slept fairly well until about 2:00am when a horrible nightmare came to him. In the dream, he was sleeping soundly but then a few small creatures, a rabbit included came up and surrounded him and he woke up but could not move. As he looked at the squirrels and birds and the rabbit, he saw they all were bleeding. Then, as they came in closer to him, they started to eat and peck at him until he was bleeding and about to die. It all seemed so real. He tried to thrash around and scare off the animals, but he was totally paralyzed and the emotional pain of seeing these things he had killed was unbelievable. The only thing he had that could do him any good was his voice, and when he screamed as loud as he could, the assailants fled.

Hours later, Zack woke up but he had the worst most splitting headache he had ever had. He went down for breakfast after getting dressed and his mother was all aghast at how he looked. He looked as though he hadn't slept at all and he was white as a sheet. After giving him his bacon and eggs, she put her hand on his forehead and said,

"Zack, are you feeling well enough to go to school?"

"I don't know, Mom. I didn't sleep too good last night. I had this bad dream and I couldn't wake up from it. Then I woke up with the worst headache I ever had."

"You know, I think I might have heard you yell last night. You haven't been experimenting with drugs have you?"

"No way, Mom. I would never do that. But actually now that you mention it, if you have some acetaminophen I think I could use a pill or two."

"I think you need a bit more care than that. I'm going to call the doctor and have him take a look at you. Good thing I'm not working today. In the meantime, go back to bed after you finish your breakfast. I'll call the school as well. This could be serious."

"Well, I don't mind staying home from school but I'm not going back to sleep until we see the doc, Mom, okay?"

"Whatever. I just spent four years in nursing school, what do I know?" After lunch, Zack persuaded his Mom to let him drive himself to the medical clinic to see their family doctor, Dr. Hendrick. The doctor was a very kind older gentleman who had gone to the four corners of the world doing free work for the poor, inside and outside Canada and was really one of the most incredible people Zack new. It was such a shame, he thought to himself that this time he really was sick. After a wait of about an hour, he was called in to an examination room. Minutes later, the Doctor arrived, with a smile on his face.

"Zack, my boy, how are they treating you in high school?" He asked

"Oh, good as ever. This is my last year so I'm not going to play football."

"Smart move, my boy. Too many concussions in football. Makes it hard to study. Even shortens the life span. So what may I ask brings you into my clinic today?"

"Well, I had this terrible dream so real that I just about woke up screaming and then when I did wake up I didn't feel rested, and I had the worst headache of my life." As he spoke, Doctor Hendrick lifted each of Zack's eyelids and peered at them then lifted his mid-length hair to look into his ears.

"Zack, my boy, I hate to say this but I think you've gone completely insane."

"You said that last time and the time before, Doctor. One of these days can you get some fresh material?" Zack replied.

"Okay, okay. Don't have to beat a dead horse, I guess. So, what have you done lately that might have caused this headache? Did you fall or hit your head? Have you been able to eat right? Fill me in."

"Well, I went hunting yesterday and I got a rabbit."

"Oh, good show! Are you going to save the pelts for gloves or maybe a lot of them for a blanket or a throw?" Doctor Hendrick asked.

"Oh no. I just shoot animals for target practice." The physician's face dropped.

"That's terrible. Don't you know those poor creatures have families and souls and such?"

"You're not serious are you? I happen to know you're a hunter yourself."

"Oh yes, I worked on a reserve for some time. Did a lot of hunting. Still do. But you see, the Native people here, and, amazingly, many in Africa feel that it is okay to kill something, big or small, but only when you are going to use that animal for something. Don't you believe that all creatures have souls?"

"I suppose, but I never saw it that way. I just wanted to practise for when I join the army."

"Zack, I have to say that if you join the army and ever kill someone it will be worse. Unless you really have no choice in the matter."

"Well, I'm going to think about that a lot, I promise I will, but in the meantime, can you give me anything for my headache?"

"I'll write out a prescription that should take care of it. As for the dreams, I don't really know what I can do. Sometimes it helps if you take a multivitamin before sleep, sometimes antihistamine works. If it still bothers you in a week, I'll send you to a specialist. Here's your prescription, be careful with these. Just take one at a time and no more than four a day."

"Thanks, Doc. I will."

Zack stopped off at the pharmacy in the same building as the clinic and got his pills, then decided he should go home to bed before taking one. He drove home thinking a lot about that rabbit he had killed, and the squirrels and stuff. He thought right back to watching movies about animals and how much he had loved his old cat. How he got to be unthinking about them he didn't know. For a while he thought it might have to do with being older and trying to be the tough guy at school showing off for the younger guys. As he got home, he left a note for his Mom and took a pill and went to bed, hoping those dreams wouldn't come back.

Zack was asleep for quite a few hours when another dream came to him. In this dream, he was a hunter from a tribe of primitive Africans, living as they had for thousands of years. Him and his tribe-mates were preparing to go out and hunt down an elephant, chanting and dancing in the way of their ancestors around a fire, putting paint and tattoos on themselves. The feeling of such primal camaraderie and the communal need for the meat the kill would bring in was another feeling that seemed to eclipse any feeling he had for hunting or shooting ever before. But then, as the hunters were preparing, an enemy tribe attacked and by some random piece of bad luck a spear went right through Zack, with the pain as real as when he was paralyzed the night before. But the attack did not kill him. Again he was on the ground, bleeding and unable to defend himself. Hours went by as he lay in that spot and all manner of birds and carrion eaters gathered to feast on his corpse. This time he was able to shake himself awake by shuffling back and forth and by realizing that despite all the pain, this was just a dream. The first thing he did was get dressed, find his flashlight, his hunting knife, and his folding shovel and left the house without leaving word to anyone. His headache was worse than ever but he didn't want to take any chances driving on the pills the Doctor had prescribed for him so, in a state of great pain, he walked out of town, trying to find where he had stopped before.

After some searching and a couple of wrong guesses, Zack finally found the place where he had parked and entered the forest. He went in, searching for a clearing that he was lucky to have found in the daytime. On and on he went, searching, following wrong path after wrong path. He envied the rich people who could afford GPS's but he had always felt his own dead reckoning was better than any electronic device. As the sun started to rise, a sprinkling of rain began and Zack's whole mind clicked into the mind of the hunter. The only difference was that now he was hunting something already dead.

As the rain kept on, soaking Zack to the bone, he was somehow able to smell the now decaying rabbit flesh. As soon as that was possible, he just followed his nose, and, in twenty minutes, he was in the clearing that he remembered. He shone his dimming flashlight, and kicked around in the grass and bushes for anything that resembled a dead rabbit that had been left to bleed with two bullets in him. As Zack searched, the rain started to slow and the sun was coming out and suddenly he found the poor little thing's remains. He pulled out his hunting knife, made four cuts around the limbs with it, then four more towards the center of the rabbit's underbelly, then pulled off the skin and tried to peel off the pelt as best he could. Then he pulled out a small folding camp stove that used flammable bars to cook things and lit it up, then took a stick and impaled the rabbit.

Zack held the bunny over the flame as the rain came down lightly, cooking it bit by bit, wondering if he really could spend the rest of his life like this as a soldier. He was tired, his head hurt and we was wet, and his parents must have been freaking out by now. The only good thing was that despite the time since it died, the rabbit meat smelled pretty good over his small fire. Soon came time to eat, and the meat tasted really good despite not having sauce, side dish or salt for it. He was a bit rusty, but after he ate all the meat, he buried the bones and said a small prayer of thanks over the makeshift grave. Now the sun had come out in full force and the rain had completely stopped. Zack looked up to see that there was a rainbow above him. He had once heard somewhere that a rainbow was a sign from God. Then he suddenly realized that his headache had gone away. This was as close to a spiritual experience that Zack had ever known, and it changed him, forever. He was never to shoot a gun again, and after spending some time making up excuses to go and talk to his Doctor, he made up his mind that after all was said and done, he would rather be a missionary than a soldier.

NIGHT FLIGHT OVER FORTRESS EUROPE

It was a chilly summer night at the Southern England Air Base in July of 1942. Frank Hereford sat in his private quarters, reading over the specifications and other information with regards to the new Spitfire mark ix he was going to fly at any given moment. He was waiting to be given orders and though he had a good idea of what they were going to be, secrecy had to be kept until the very last moment.

Flying was a game Frank knew well. He had been at it for fifteen of his 35 years. Wealthy parents and a lust to navigate the skies allowed him to pursue his goal of being a top-notch pilot when most people in England were lining up for soup or other handouts. It was not a fair system, but now that most of those soup-eaters were able to keep two feet on the ground and live in relative safety compared to him, flying missions all over Europe, his life at the mercy of his own skill versus that of the enemy, he felt as though justice had been served.

Commander Hereford was actually quite pleased at the specifications about the new Spit. It looked like it could fly faster and turn quicker than the ME109 and even the German's newer plane, the FW190. He was a bit ticked off that there would be no chance for him to test fly the plane. He was simply given manuals and expected to react to flying it as if he had been flying it all along. This was something that could get dangerous, especially if aerial combat was a possibility.

As he was admiring the new plane and mentally going through what it would be like to pull a fast turn on a German plane and move in for the kill in it, a knock came at the door. He had known it would be coming, but he would have much rather been sleeping the night away and waking up next to his wife than having to fly another mission. His stomach tightened and he felt the taste of bile in his throat, despite the fact that, with his experience, he was possibly the most deadly ace in England.

"Commander Hereford, Sir?" Came the voice with the knock.

Frank opened the door to see Thompson, one of the brighter young LAC's he had taken up in two-seaters and had more than once thought of recommending for flight training. They said he was too young and hadn't completed his secondary school so Britain would have to pass on another candidate for the one big thing they lacked: pilots.

"Yes, Thompson, what is it?" He said in a bit of an annoyed tone. He knew he was going to be summoned but this was his own way of sounding off that he didn't like being chosen for these tricky assignments that always turned out to be dangerous. It didn't do him any good, but it often kept people edgy when they were around him, especially the lower ranks, which he liked to do. To him, this was one of the God-given privileges that officers had over lower ranks.

"I have orders for you, Sir, from the Squadron Leader," Thompson replied, being careful not to let on that the Commander made him nervous.

"Very well, very well. Give them to me and don't stand there like I'm going to tip you."

"Sorry Sir. My instructions are to give you the orders and watch you destroy them."

"I suppose burning would be good enough."

"That would be what was intended in the order, Sir."

"Well, I don't smoke man. What am I supposed to do, eat them?" Thompson handed Commander Hereford his own lighter and took a step back from the door without closing it. The orders read as follows:

COMMANDER HEREFORD, EYES ONLY.

YOU ARE TO TAKE THE NEW SPITFIRE MARK IX

FLY IT TO THE AREA MARKED ON THE MAP

SEEK OUT THE STRUCTURE DRAWN BELOW

TAKE AS MANY PICTURES AS YOU CAN OF IT

THEN RETURN TO BASE IN A CIRCUITOUS ROUTE

YOU ARE NOT TO ENGAGE THE ENEMY

UNLESS YOU ARE FORCED TO

Commander Hereford took a long look at the map and then set flame to both documents. He made sure they burned completely and put them into an empty waste basket. Then he dismissed Thompson and made his way to the pilot's locker room to get into his flight gear.

Hereford knew what they were after. Many planes and lives had been lost going after the same thing. The Germans had been making rockets, and if they were allowed to complete their plans the entire balance of power could be easily changed between the Allies and Axis powers. Once he got his gear in order, he made his way to the intelligence building and had a long chat with his friend Archie about German anti-aircraft emplacements and the various airfields that could be alerted to his presence. He had become one of the top pilots in the RAF by his incredible memory and devotion to every detail of each mission, not to mention his skill and marksmanship. This had also made him part of an even smaller class of men, one of the top live pilots in the RAF.

Soon after his all-too brief briefing, he had climbed into the cockpit of the new Spitfire and was quickly told what to expect once he got the plane in the air and how the camera worked. With a crisp salute and smile, Frank was taxiing down the runway to a new adventure he really wished he could have let someone else experience.

///

It felt good. It felt renewing to push the throttle handle forward and guide the aircraft's tail up, then cautiously lift it off the main wheels and take to the air, retracting the wheels for greater speed and lift and freeing itself from all the bounds of the Earth. This was the part of flying Frank loved the most, before he had spent all his effort and skill on the completion of a mission, before his plane was shot up and nearly out of gas or the wheels were leaking hydraulic fluid forcing him to land belly-up. He decided he was going to fly south west until he hit Cornwall and then lower his altitude greatly and try to sneak past any German patrols by roughly following the outline of France over the water. A more direct route would take him over Normandy where a plethora of German airborne and land-based defenses would almost surely pepper him with everything they had. Those were the facts though: most of the missions he and his squadron mates were sent on were out over that area, and any pictures or intelligence achieved was like gold. Both the Germans and the Allies wanted to find out as much as they could about the Normandy and surrounding coastal area because soon there would have to be an invasion. Little did they know that the invasion would be useless if the rocket building areas and launches weren't kept in check or, with any luck, destroyed.

Out over the water, a million stars shone above him and the moon was just over the horizon. It looked so huge there and it sent out a lot of soft yellow light. It was risky to send a mission at this time when the moon was full, but the planners back home had hoped the extra light could possibly illuminate a target that he would be photographing. He could take pictures in the dark, but as far as finding something worth taking picture of, that was another problem. This was an incredibly important, super-secret mission, but it was also incredibly dangerous and most likely useless. He had flown these 'rocket-finding' missions before and he had yet to see anything but the enemy aircraft he was forced to destroy. Frank had likely shot down more than 30 enemy planes, but he wasn't decorated or even recognized as doing so because it was so important to keep his missions quiet.

After a little more than an hour or flying out over the water, Commander Hereford turned his lithe and powerful Spitfire into land and headed to some industrial and farm country to the south of Bordeaux. He mentally calculated, with the help of the instrument cluster in the Spit how long it would take for him to check out the area in question. Then, he took his altitude down to tree-top level in hopes that he could evade more threats in that way. Certainly, lower level flights would avoid radar, but if this was a rocket site, it would most likely give itself away by being doubly fortified with anti-aircraft guns and patrols of German fighters. As he drew in closer it seemed to him that this was just another falsely acquired piece of intelligence.

Frank neared the target and, as he pulled back on the stick and gained altitude, he thought of his young wife who had hopefully long since gone to bed and what would happen if he didn't come home from a mission. He loved her dearly and they had hoped to have a child or two one day. It made him sick to think of raising a child when such brutality and destruction existed. Years back, when the war started, it seemed he was a thousand years younger, he was so eager to sign up, so full of piss and wind about how he and his squadron would fly to glory over Germany. The battle of Britain claimed the lived of 60% of his original squadron and most of the ones that survived that were lost in bomber escort missions over Germany. Even after all that, Frank had decided that he would personally give everything he could of himself to end the war or die trying, so he requested a transfer to intelligence and here he was. So many people had cheered on the aviators when the Battle of Britain ended. Fact was that when the sirens used to go off, it was very common to see men vomiting from the incredible strain it took on them to fly two, three sorties a day facing down wave after wave of enemies, knowing that each time they failed to nail a bomber or fighter someone would die either in another aircraft or from having a bomb drop on them. He remembered landing after pitched battles, he and the other men counting the returning planes, hoping all of them made it, knowing that most of the free world was watching, too.

Still, somehow as Frank was executing a climbing turn, keeping his eyes peeled at ever little abnormality or such as he checked out the area, still this was an enjoyable thing to do. The good feeling lasted for about 27 seconds. He was taking the last of the pictures he was going to take and he came around to spot two Me109's turning to engage him.

As a trick to see if they had spotted him, the Commander flipped his Spitfire over in a belly-up position, and dropped down to around 100 feet from the1,500 feet he was taking photos from. It was harder to spot the plane upside down, though few pilots had the skill, it was a trick that often worked. This time it didn't.

One of the 109's was able to spot him and he left the second German plane to cover him while he dove after Frank's Spit. Frank flipped over and put the throttles to full and dropped down even lower. While he was gaining speed, the first 109 being in a dive, there was a brief moment when the enemy had him in his sights and the enemy took full advantage, pouring a staccato stream of 20mm cannon rounds from its two nose cannons into Hereford's plane. Frank responded by pulling up, reducing throttle and putting the Spitfire into a sharp left-hand turn with 60% flaps. The Messerschmitt responded by diving down and trying to copy and outdo the Spitfire but the Me109's weren't nearly as good at turns as the Mark IX's. They went through a number of circles, and, at the end of the third, Frank had the German dead to rights. He unleashed the power of his own guns and must have hit a fuel line because the plane exploded in the air, and the pilot had no chance to get out and use his chute.

For a moment, Frank thought he was in the clear, but then he realized there had been two 109's. He closed his eyes for a moment and before he opened them, he once again heard the staccato rhythm of twin 20 mm cannons going off, ripping out most of his rudder, something he would need to return to England. Most pilots at this time would have opened up their canopy and jumped, but, instead, Frank pulled back his stick and went straight up, where the enemy plane could hear him but hopefully not see him. He then completed the manoeuver by completing a loop and ended up right behind and above the German, and let loose on him until his right wing broke off, which actually took just seconds. In the reality of aerial combat though, mere seconds can be your life expectancy if you don't learn fast to hit hard and run. This time, the pilot got out and his parachute opened. This was another thing about the gallantry of the skies, which was being done less and less as this frightening war continued. If at all possible, a fighter pilot will take out the plane instead of the man.

//

The kill was good. It actually had left Commander Hereford with an immense feeling of satisfaction. Unfortunately, the fight had also left him without a portion of his tail rudder. He could still steer, the damaged control surface wasn't completely gone, and a plane actually didn't turn with just a rudder. He was going to have problems getting his damaged Spit back to England because he would only be able to make awkward turns and if there was a rough wind when he went to land, just using his ailerons was going to make things difficult. But Hereford had been through difficult landings before.

There had been one landing where he had just ounces of fuel left in his tanks and he was being pursued by a FW190, a nasty German plane for anyone to knock out of the sky. He wasn't far from his airfield, but he was leading this plane right to its location where it would more than likely take out a number of targets before they could even leave the ground. Luckily though, he was able to establish radio contact and let his boys know this plane was coming and that he would be in front of it, desperate to land. He streaked over the airfield and pulled up for altitude, which he would need for the landing, but in the eyes of the German pursuing him would be suicide, but as the German pulled up to move in for the kill, the full force of the airfield's anti-aircraft batteries let loose and annihilated the German plane. The pilot got out, however, and despite a wound in his leg from the flak that downed him, he was an amiable sort. He was quite happy when he had heard that he would be sent to Canada as he had been fascinated more with the Democracy among plenty that the Country seemed to be about that he had for a long time wanted to go there. Hereford even sat him down while they were waiting for the Military Police to come and pick him up and drank most of a bottle of Johnny Walker Red label with him. For the German pilot the war was over; for Frank it was just beginning.

There wasn't going to be much hope of a rescue like that one he had pulled over his own airfield with the amiable German though, his plan was to top out the plane's optimum altitude and speed capability and run hell for leather at over 400 mph at the altitude of 25,000 feet the manual had said was the plane's optimum. At that speed, it could outrun just about anything in the sky. He strongly hoped the few things he couldn't outrun would be down for maintenance on that particular night.

Twice as he headed for home that night a German plane had spotted him and both times they simply had no way of keeping up with him. The Mark IX was just too fast. He was able to get on the radio and establish contact with an airfield just past the waters of the English channel, but as he neared the end of France over Normandy, he spotted an enemy squadron of bombers and fighters headed right at him, guns blazing, possibly alerted of his presence by spotters on the ground.

The Commander took a number of hits to his plane, leaving his engine coughing smoke and slowing his speed greatly. By a grand stroke of luck, a flight of American P-51 Mustangs had been sent up to pursue the bombers and fighters, and the fact that these German planes were now turning to try and down Commander Hereford was going to make the Mustang pilots' job much easier. One of the American pilots peeled away from the formation and took it upon himself to escort Frank back to the airfield he was headed for. "God bless those yanks." Frank said to himself. "Maybe one day I will even forgive them for being late in joining this bloody war."

Having lost most of his power, and a good bit of his maneuverability, Frank decided the best thing he could do would be to gain altitude. The Spitfire could glide quite a way on no power, and with a smoking engine that could catch fire at any time, the soonest possible chance he could get to shut off the engine would be the safest. Not to mention that he really didn't want to end up in the freezing waters of the English Channel, rescue boat on its way or no. He climbed all he could. Then when he had estimated he could come in to where the airfield was located and have a safety margin to over-fly the airport and get an idea of how it lay and which way the wind was blowing, he shut down the Rolls Royce engine that had brought him all this way and said a silent prayer to himself, the one he normally saved for roulette and cards.

As Frank sat there in the relative calm and silence of the still early morning sky over the Channel, a feeling of peace came over him. He remembered as a child what his brother would say when a peaceful, serene moment would come like this one, "I'm so relaxed I could shit." Funny how things like that come up. His brother had been in America after the previous war and had died in the flu pandemic that had killed at least as many people of the Great War. That was so long ago, yet there were times when Frank would reach for a sheet of stationary to write him a letter and in the reaching remember he was gone.

More important things than memories were pressing on his mind, as now he had glided down to 5,000 feet. The American plane had left him to his own devices now, leaving with a crisp salute and a victory roll, as the airfield was now coming into view. It looked like a rough and barely used field, with the odd wrecked truck or burned out plane near the runway. This could have been one of the earlier fields of the war, now abandoned except for skeleton staff that were there to help bring in damaged aircraft from missions gone wrong.

Although it looked like he had estimated the altitude he would need to glide in was wrong, the extra space he had allotted to check out the field would not be needed since he had gotten a visual confirmation so quickly as to where he would be setting down. He was coming in fast, feeling that he was going to hit hard if he tried to land at this speed, so he instinctively pulled back on the stick and slowed the Spitfire, which made it harder for him to keep the plane going in a straight and level forward motion. The controls of a plane in the cockpit can do three things, go up and down, with the use of the horizontal stabilizer in the tail, go left and right with the help of the tail rudder, which was now shot off, and roll right or left with the ailerons which are in the main wings.

As Frank was trying to keep his plane going slow enough to safely touch down, he could only do two of these things. When you turn a plane, you need to co-ordinate the tail rudder, using your two foot pedals and the roll function which is done with the left-right movement of the control stick. You can turn with only the left-right movement of the stick, but it is awkward and extremely difficult to make a landing like that. This particular landing would be a rough one.

There was no wind to speak of, which would work in Frank's favor, though his heart seemed to beat faster and faster with each yard he got closer to the runway. In one instance as he drew in he over-controlled and his plane went back and forth as he tried to right it and had to fight and unlearn how to turn with rudders. He lowered his flaps as he eased through 1,500 feet, which are the two 'flaps' of moveable control surface on the inside part of each wing. Lowering them meant turning a crank which kept them in one spot, causing air to move faster over the top of the inside of the wing and slower over the bottom, giving more lift at lower speeds. He had delayed this action to 1,500 feet because, though it made it easier to fly a slow-moving plane, it drew from the plane's inertia or 'forward-moving force' and this was something Frank was low on. He was slowing down just slightly too fast.

The seconds ticked by, Frank kept a close eye on the wind sock. A sudden gust could send him off course, and that would be a disaster at the least. He was tense everywhere, but then he remembered that he had done this in training and the real thing before, he relaxed his grip on the flight stick, took a deep breath and let himself fly by instinct. In he came, his main wheels touching down just at the edge of the runway. It was quite a bumpy ride, as this airfield seemed to have not been maintained in any special manner, but he did touch down. For seemingly no reason whatsoever, Commander Hereford laughed to himself, maybe because he had cheated the Gods one more time.

After his main wheels were down and he felt the aircraft was stable, he let down the tail section which had remained in the air for the first part of the landing as one must do with any 'tail dragger'. That was where the problem came in. When a small plane touches down, being at a higher speed, it is first kept moving in a straight line down the runway by ailerons, the main-wing control surfaces. As it slows, most such aircraft have brakes, which are at the tip of the rudder controls on the floor. Using his skill gained in training, you mainly guide the aircraft down the runway with rudders and brakes in the final part of the landing. When Frank slowed, he hit a bump or a stone on the right hand wheel and when he tried to recover instinctively, he turned and the speed of his plane caused it to tip. Now there was nothing he could do. He had sincerely hoped to bring this Spitfire back in one piece, as it had been nice enough to reciprocate for him. Now he had to deal with something every pilot fears: Fire!

His smoking engine must have been leaking fuel, which was ignited somehow in the flipping over. There was no rush of sirens, no emergency vehicles to come in and save him. He would have to get out on his own. He struggled with the canopy and it didn't want to budge under the strength of his arms or even his will. Frank Hereford was not a man to give up easy, so he turned himself upside down, took out his pistol and fired three shots at one of the thick canopy windows, then kicked at it for all he was worth. Somehow it popped out and he tried to exit the cockpit through the hole but had no luck. He decided he himself could fit but not his flight gear and clothing. He took out a knife from his pocket and, as the flames grew around him, he cut off what he couldn't struggle out of until he was stripped down to his long underwear. He then tried again and managed to squeeze out most of himself. Now, a jeep had arrived and came to help him try and escape the burning wreck. The two of them working together, got him out, though the flames and spitting oil did a good job on what was left of Frank's uniform.

The two of them scrambled away, knowing the plane could blow up at any minute. Then Frank and the Sergeant who had just saved his life sat on the grass, enjoying a brief respite from the insanity of the war. In around two more minutes, the Spitfire blew, and the two just watched, laughing at the fate that had brought the two away from the burning wreck just in time. The Sergeant, a Canadian offered a suggestion that they should get some sausages from the mess to cook over the fire.

"If it wasn't an oil fire, I would agree with you. Say, what normally happens when a pilot lands here at this time of night?"

"Well, I billet him in that building, " He said, pointing to a comfortable looking pre-fabricated structure. "Then in a day or two they send someone to get you."

"Two days, eh! Any liquor about?"

"I keep a fair sized stash in my quarters, yes."

"Well then, Sergeant, you and I are going to have a good time getting to know each other. Sometimes it seems I haven't had a good drink since this bloody war started."

"I know exactly how you feel, Sir. I'll get you some coveralls from the mechanic's stores. Then we'll sit down by the wireless and toast the fact that we lived to fight another day."

"Sergeant, I get the feeling with a recommendation I'm going to make you're in for a medal and a promotion, maybe a posting away from this little lump of Earth."

"Promotion or no Sir, I'll still have to charge you for the booze, stuff is bleeding hard to get around here."

"Cheap bastard."

"It's the War Sir, it's the bloody War."

The End

Made in the USA
Charleston, SC
17 May 2013